IMPACTFUL COMMUNITY-BASED
LITERACY PROJECTS

D1570209

IMPACTFUL COMMUNITY-BASED LITERACY PROJECTS

LESLEY S. J. FARMER

FOREWORD BY
LOIS BRIDGES

CHICAGO   2021

Lesley S. J. Farmer, professor at California State University, Long Beach (CSULB), coordinates the Teacher Librarian Program and manages the CSU Information and Communication Technology (ICT) Literacy Project. She earned her MS in library science at the University of North Carolina, Chapel Hill, and received her doctorate in adult education from Temple University. Farmer has worked as a librarian in K–12 school settings as well as in public, special, and academic libraries. She chaired the Special Libraries Association's Education Divisions and IFLA's School Library Section. Farmer is a Fulbright scholar and has received national and international grants. She has also been honored with several professional association awards, including the Ken Haycock Award for Promoting Librarianship. Farmer's research interests include ICT, media literacies, and data analytics. A frequent presenter and writer for the profession, Farmer has published three dozen professional books and more than two hundred professional book chapters and articles.

Extensive effort has gone into ensuring the reliability of the information in this book; however, the publisher makes no warranty, express or implied, with respect to the material contained herein.

ISBN: 978-0-8389-4803-3 (paper)

Library of Congress Cataloging-in-Publication Data

Names: Farmer, Lesley S. J., author.
Title: Impactful community-based literacy projects / Lesley S. J. Farmer ; foreword by Lois Bridges.
Description: Chicago : ALA Editions, 2021. | Includes bibliographical references and index. | Summary: "This book addresses trends in literacy efforts and provides guidance for developing, implementing and assessing impactful community-based literacy projects"—Provided by publisher.
Identifiers: LCCN 2020025998 | ISBN 9780838948033 (Paperback : acid-free paper)
Subjects: LCSH: Literacy—Social aspects. | Literacy programs. | Communication in social action.
Classification: LCC LC149 .F37 2020 | DDC 372.6—dc23
LC record available at https://lccn.loc.gov/2020025998

Text design in the Chaparral, Gotham, and Bell Gothic typefaces. Cover design by Alejandra Diaz. Images © Adobe Stock.

♾ This paper meets the requirements of ANSI/NISO Z39.48-1992 (Permanence of Paper).

Printed in the United States of America
25 24 23 22 21   5 4 3 2 1

Contents

Foreword

Literacy Is Life

In 2013, the philanthropist David M. Rubenstein established the Library of Congress Literacy Awards Program to "honor nonprofit organizations that have made outstanding contributions to increasing literacy in the United States or abroad." In this way, the awards illuminate the importance of literacy while also showcasing and disseminating innovative and effective methods across the states and around the world that promote literacy.

Like the awards that inspired her book, the goal of professor of education and library science scholar Lesley Farmer is to "facilitate worldwide literacy." Not only has she created a compendium of Literacy Awards winners, providing a helpful overview of each winning project, she also embeds each project within a frame of "community literacy"—noting that the most effective and sustainable projects share a commitment to community-based needs and participation.

While the first thing we may think when we hear the term *literacy* is early reading and the ABCs, Farmer makes clear that literacy is much more than foundational reading skills. For one thing, literacy has innumerable manifestations. The term transcends print and now includes media, health, and information as well as cultural, fiscal, ecological, emotional, and recreational literacy. Clearly, literacy is multifaceted and shaped by the context in which it occurs. Each specialized literacy represents a constellation of highly specific and often complex knowledge. As Farmer notes of health literacy, it "may be as simple as reading food and medical labels and as complicated as determining health insurance options."

And if we examine the United Nations' *2030 Agenda for Sustainable Development*, as Farmer does, we see the broad impact of literacy. This United Nations Agenda includes seventeen goals, which provide a road map for our survival—everything from ending poverty and hunger to providing sustainable housing. Achieving all seventeen depends on robust literacy.

Given the importance of literacy to our lives, Farmer's exploration of the many functions and manifestations of literacy is both alluring and helpful. Farmer also includes a practical guide to initiating your own literacy project. How do you plan a literacy project, conduct a needs assessment, establish the goals and objectives of your literacy project, and identify and target your audience? What does the research say about productive literacy partnerships? Farmer helps detail the steps needed to create an effective and sustaining project in your own community.

Ultimately, Farmer's book is likely to spark a deeper understanding of literacy in its most exalted state: as a tool for self-discovery; for development of the mind and heart; literacy to develop the intellect and knowledge of the world; literacy for liberation. This is the indispensable role of literacy we need to embrace in our schools, in our communities, and in our civic life.

Farmer serves on the Library of Congress Literacy Awards Board. She is well acquainted with deeply compelling efforts underway across our states and around the world to make literacy accessible to all. As you read her book, you will revel in the many manifestations of literacy around the globe—and the projects in place meant to promote literacy. Consider choosing one or more to support—or, using Farmer's blueprint as your guide, create your own. Our lives depend on literacy. Indeed, as Farmer suggests, literacy is life.

—DR. LOIS BRIDGES, VICE PRESIDENT AND
PUBLISHER, SCHOLASTIC PROFESSIONAL

Introduction

Words, words, words! They are all around us: in signs, in mass media, in stores, in the workplace, online, at school, in games. The effective use of language is vital for communication and is the basis for literacy. As such, literacy constitutes a basic learning need and is considered a foundational skill for civilization. Literacy enables people to access and comprehend information that helps them participate effectively in their societies. Nevertheless, literacy is not easy to define. Nor is literacy a universal ability.

UNESCO (2004) defines literacy as

> the ability to identify, understand, interpret, create, communicate and compute, using printed and written (and visual) materials associated with varying contexts. Literacy involves a continuum of learning in enabling individuals to achieve their goals, to develop their knowledge and potential, and to participate fully in their community and wider society (p. 13).

The term *literacy* takes on different connotations when translated (UNESCO, 2006). For instance, in several countries the term is generally *alphabétisme*, which seems to limit the concept to one of a writing system, such as learning one's ABCs. Other nations associate literacy with the three Rs: reading, writing and arithmetic. France uses the term *littérisme* to describe what is often defined as *functional literacy*: the ability to read and write simple text for everyday life—which leads into UNESCO's more advanced definition, adopted in 1978:

> A person is functionally literate who can engage in all those activities in which literacy is required for effective functioning of his group and community and also for enabling him to continue to use reading, writing and calculation for his own and the community's development (p. 1).

In some cases, functional literacy is linked to economics or community development: a person's function within society.

In turn, people who are functionally illiterate cannot use reading, writing, and calculation to develop themselves or to engage in activities that need literacy to function. An illiterate person cannot read or write simple text for everyday life (UNESCO, 1978). Thus, functionality implies a higher level of competency.

As for people who are aliterate, they have the ability to read, but do not have the habit or desire to do so. For such people, reading is often slow and frustrating. Usually aliteracy does not address writing. It tends to occur more often in the developed world than in developing worlds (National Endowment for the Arts, 2004).

The concept of literacy has also changed over time. For instance, the term *literate* comes from the Latin word meaning "educated," "learned," or "one who knows the letters" (such as the ABCs). An underlying assumption was that literacy was associated with human-recorded information, as opposed to oral transmission. As novels became popular in the late eighteenth century, literacy was associated with acquaintance with literature. A century later, literacy signified the ability to read and write. Indeed, the concept of writing was originally not part of the definition of literacy, since writing materials were scarce; writing was a separate skill of scribes. In fact, the first recorded information was to keep inventory of merchandise. Early on, writing was used as a mnemonic to remember spoken words such as songs and drama. Nowadays, literacy may be considered as a range or continuum of communication practices that may include additional formats beyond text such as numbers and images. In fact, the term *literacy* has been used as a general catchall to mean "access, understand, use, communicate and generate" with whatever type of knowledge or format, including visual, media, digital, health, information, fiscal, ecological, cultural, emotional, and recreational.

In its conceptualization of literacy, UNESCO (2006) parsed literacy into four aspects:

- An autonomous set of reading, writing, and oral skills that build from phonetics and orthographic systems of recording knowledge; numeracy is usually considered a supplemental skill.

- Situated application, which reflects socially contextualized practice, unlike the concept of a universal, culturally neutral set of skills.
- A learning process rather than a product or result, with the idea of active, socially situated experiences of internal and external dynamics.
- Text, which focuses on subject matter, genre, and structure (e.g., newspapers versus magazines).

These perspectives reflect the complexity of literacy and acknowledge how different cultures and nations might interpret literacy. In this book, UNESCO's definition is used, focusing on textual information so as to provide a baseline of literacy initiatives.

WHY IS LITERACY IMPORTANT?

While the oral tradition continues to exist and be recorded for posterity, comprehending and acting on textual information is necessary in almost all aspects of vocational and personal success, from applying for a job to reading medicine directions.

As early as 1948, the universal right to education, including free education at the elementary or fundamental level, was expressly stated in the United Nations Declaration of Human Rights. The 1995 UNESCO Convention on the Rights of the Child specifically focused on children's education as a chief means to participate as active and responsible citizens. At that point, of the 130 million children with no access to school, 63 percent were girls.

In 2018 the International Literacy Association (ILA) asserted that children have a basic human right to read. This right also means that children have the right to access print and digital texts, and can choose what they read. They also have the right to supportive reading environments and reading instruction. The ILA considers this issue one of equity and social justice, especially as 250 million children worldwide cannot read at a basic level; the result is that these children will have fewer options in life and will be more likely to be excluded from society. Reading, the ILA says, not only improves children's critical thinking and expands their knowledge base, but it also helps them build compassion and empathy because it exposes them to different experiences and points of view.

In examining the United Nations' (2015) *2030 Agenda for Sustainable Development*, one can see the impact of literacy on the seventeen goals:

1. End poverty: access to economic resources requires literacy to use them.
2. End hunger: ensuring safe and nutritious food requires literacy to read labels, recipes, and agricultural manuals, as well as to market foods and invest in the food sector.

3. Ensure healthy lives for all: access to health information and resources requires literacy to use and communicate them.
4. Ensure quality education for all: access to information, including educational opportunities, requires literacy to gain knowledge and skills.
5. Achieve gender equity: effective participation and equal opportunities for leadership requires literacy for access to—and leveraging of—information, resources, education, and communication.
6. Ensure water and sanitation for all: effective management of water and sanitation requires literacy to access and use information and resources.
7. Ensure affordable, reliable, sustainable, and modern energy for all: access to—and management of—energy requires literacy to access and use information and resources.
8. Promote inclusive, sustainable economic growth with decent employment for all: economies need literate employees to work knowledgeably and productively.
9. Build infrastructures, promote industrialization, and innovate: increasing enterprise and providing supporting infrastructures requires literacy to develop, produce, and market goods and services.
10. Reduce inequality within and among countries: education, economic opportunities, and civic engagement requires literacy to access and leverage them.
11. Make human settlements safe and sustainable: housing, basic services, and transportation requires literacy to access, develop, and use them effectively.
12. Ensure sustainable consumption and production: managing natural resources requires literacy to access information and use it to optimize resource use.
13. Combat climate change: literacy is required to access information about climate change and have the skills to address it.
14. Conserve marine resources: managing resources and addressing adverse effects (e.g., pollution, extinction of organisms) requires literacy to access and use relevant information.
15. Manage terrestrial ecosystems: managing resources and addressing adverse effects (e.g., land degradation, extinction of organisms) requires literacy to access and use relevant information and resources.
16. Promote peace and justice: literacy is required to ensure civic participation and to promote and enforce the rule of law through access to information and effective communication.
17. Strengthen global partnership for sustainable development: literacy is required to gain expertise and resources to invest international support.

WHAT IS THE PROBLEM?

UNESCO (1958) has promoted literacy for over fifty years through its Initiative for Literacy and other campaigns. The years 2003 to 2012 were declared the United Nations Literacy Decade as a means to focus on this global issue, especially as it applies to women. While literacy rates rose 2 to 3 percent over all by 2013, nine hundred million people still lacked basic literacy skills, and the rate for women did not change.

While UNESCO's 2017 statistics about basic literacy look promising, with an 86 percent global literacy rate and a narrowing gap between men (90 percent) and women (83 percent), that still leaves 750 million illiterate persons, with women constituting 63 percent of that population. Drilling down, statistics reveal that almost half of the global illiterate population live in Southern Asia. Moreover, the majority of people in twenty countries within sub-Saharan Africa are illiterate. In those two geographic regions, women ages 15 years and older are a fifth less likely to be literate than men of the same age. On a more positive note, these areas also have witnessed the greatest increase in youth literacy over the last fifty years: an 89 percent literacy rate in Southern Asia and 75 percent in sub-Saharan Africa, both of which regions also reflect a shrinking gender gap.

Canada's Literacy Foundation (2017) succinctly summarized negative consequences of illiteracy at the levels of the individual and society as a whole. For individuals, illiteracy can lead to:

- Less ability to access and comprehend needed information, such as health advice
- Less access to lifelong learning opportunities
- Fewer options for employment, especially for higher-paid professional jobs
- An unstable financial situation
- Lower self-esteem and more loneliness
- Poorer decisions

At the societal level, illiteracy can lead to:

- Workplace vacancies for trained personnel
- Less effective use of personnel
- Lower workplace productivity
- Lower GDP
- Greater health costs
- Less civic engagement

In short, a mind is a terrible thing to waste.

WHAT IS THE SOLUTION FOR ILLITERACY?

Ah, if there were a simple, no-fail solution to illiteracy, the world would be a better place. Frankly, literacy is a complex process. Several individual preconditions are necessary for literacy: working memory, sensory and perception skills, cognitive and motor skills, even social skills. The external environment also has to support literacy: a print-rich environment with material that is developmentally appropriate and in the mother tongue. An intelligent agent has to link the person to the material and guide the reading process as well as provide opportunities and incentives to practice literacy behaviors. While literacy is often considered the job of formal education, these preconditions start as early at birth. Especially as the body is conditioned to process certain learning opportunities at optimal times, such as second-language acquisition, providing those learning experiences and appropriate support in an optimum situation can be problematic. Especially as individual characteristics, environments, and unique events shape learning, it is hard to imagine coordinating these conditions on a national or international scale.

WHAT IS A COMMUNITY?

No perfect scenario actually exists. However, identifying and optimizing conditions that facilitate—and impede—literacy are key. Providing opportunities to access reading materials is key. Providing trained personnel to support the reading process is key. Motivating individuals to learn how to read is key. Providing incentives and opportunities to practice and improve literacy behaviors is key. All of these issues exist within situational and cultural contexts, at the same time valuing and empowering individuals to make positive literacy decisions. While society cannot control any individual completely (nor should it), it can provide a choice of material and human resources that align with and support individual choice and action. Such efforts can be done systematically to help the largest applicable population possible. Here is where models of effective literacy efforts come into play. And here is where community makes a critical difference.

What, then, is a community? It consists of people with characteristics in common, be they locational (such as a neighborhood or online game), cognitive (such as interests), or psychological (such as culture or values). Cultures, be they a social group or a profession, have a set of norms, beliefs, and institutions. In contrast, a community reflects a localized set of relationships and shared assets within a particularized environment. Community-based literacy efforts have a better chance of succeeding because they are not mandated from an outside body or a group that does not understand or have power within the community. A community-based effort not only provides the environment and expertise for literacy education, but it also provides authentic opportunities to practice literacy behaviors and to support and guide those behaviors.

For these reasons, this book focuses on community-based literacy efforts.

HOW THIS GUIDE CAN HELP

This book was inspired by the Library of Congress Literacy Awards Program and its applicants. Each year the applications are analyzed to discern trends and identify factors that distinguish honored projects from other efforts. The analysis also collates the research that grounds the projects, which then builds the conceptual foundation for future literacy initiatives (Library of Congress, 2019).

These projects and accompanying analyses offer proven practices that can facilitate new literacy projects around the world. More specifically, one of the factors that was common to most effective and sustainable literacy projects was community-based needs and participation. Therefore, this book focuses on these kinds of literacy efforts. To this end, the book promotes blending universal findings such as early literacy benefits and fundamental reading skills along with culture- or community-specific sensitivity and leveraging to optimize results.

Chapter 1 explains universal steps to literacy: how people learn, generic reading skill development, human developmental issues, and habits of literacy.

Chapter 2 outlines literacy projects in terms of their characteristics and discusses research-based factors for impactful literacy projects.

Chapter 3 focuses on literacy partners, starting by discussing the nature of groups and the basics of partnerships. Then it describes specific types of partners: families, schools and universities, libraries, government agencies, nonprofit organizations, and for-profit entities.

Chapter 4 details a variety of literacy issues: personal, social and community-based, cultural, linguistic, educational, technological, economic, and political/governmental.

Chapter 5 discusses associated applied literacies: health, fiscal, environmental, media, and cultural.

Chapter 6 details how to plan literacy projects, starting an action research approach. It gives advice about planners, needs assessment, goals and objectives, literacy review, target audience, project personnel, resources, setting and timing, communication, support, implementation, communication, and continuous assessment and improvement.

The conclusion suggests next steps: building capacity, empowering the community, and sustaining a culture of literacy.

Sample community-based literacy projects from Library of Congress Literacy Awards honorees and representative resources are found throughout the book.

The fundamental hope and goal of this book is to facilitate worldwide literacy. Each person has the ability to contribute to this effort, and together we can succeed.

REFERENCES

International Literacy Association. (2018). *The case for children's rights to read.* Newark, DE: International Literacy Association.

Library of Congress. (2019). *About the library.* Washington, DC: Library of Congress.

Literacy Foundation. (2017). *Consequences of illiteracy.* Montreal, Canada: Literacy Foundation.

National Endowment for the Arts. (2004). *Reading at risk: A survey of literary reading in America.* Washington, DC: National Endowment for the Arts.

UNESCO. (2017). *UIS fact sheet no. 45.* Paris: UNESCO.

UNESCO. (2006). *Education for all global monitoring report.* Paris: UNESCO.

UNESCO. (2004). *The plurality of literacy and its implications for policies and programmes.* Paris: UNESCO.

UNESCO. (1995). *The Convention on the Rights of the Child.* Paris: UNESCO.

UNESCO. (1978). *Revised recommendation concerning the international standardization of educational statistics.* Paris: UNESCO.

UNESCO. (1958). *Recommendation concerning the international standardization of educational statistics.* Paris: UNESCO.

United Nations. (2015). *Transforming our world: The 2030 Agenda for Sustainable Development.* The Hague: United Nations.

United Nations. (1948). *The universal declaration of human rights.* The Hague: United Nations.

1

Steps to Literacy

Understanding how literacy is acquired can help communities optimize their efforts. As mentioned in the introduction, literacy is a strictly human endeavor of conscious learning. It reflects a complex set of skills that involve several parts of the brain, sensory organs, motor skills, and emotions. Even with UNESCO's broad definition of literacy, reading remains the foundation skill. Therefore, this chapter discusses the general elements of learning, and then focuses on learning how to be literate in terms of reading. Literacy is a lifelong activity that reflects human development changes, so these factors are also addressed.

HOW PEOPLE LEARN

What is learning? Fundamentally, learning consists of change: of disposition and behavior. Learning requires accepting new information and integrating it into existing personal mental schemata, which can be acted on. From the day of birth, people learn, sensing and interacting with their environments. Technically, people can learn until the day they die. While learning is often associated with formal education, potentially it can happen anywhere, anytime. In every case, though, all individuals are ultimately responsible for their own learning in that no one else can learn for them. Learning is truly a self-monitoring activity that changes over time.

For learning to take place, individuals have to sense and perceive the information from the external environment, be able to process it internally, and act on it. Learning involves the brain's sensory cortex in getting information, the nearby integrative cortex for making meaning of information, the frontal integrative cortex that creates new ideas from the meaning, and the motor context, which acts on the ideas. Learning also changes the brain by practice as neurons connect and grow through repetition. Neurons signal connections called synapses, which are strengthened via chemicals that effect the emotions. The body's feelings differ with the cognitive experience, from pleasure to despair, so teachers should try to stimulate positive feelings by appealing to potential learners' interests and aiming for satisfying experiences (Zull, 2004).

In addition, several theories explain how people learn, taking into account the environment and the people therein (Tompkins, 2018). *Constructivist learning theories* posit that individuals are motivated and active learners, that they relate new information to prior learning, and that they organize and integrate information in schemata. *Interactive learning theories* focus on what people do: they read, drawing on prior knowledge as they read text and use word-recognition skills and comprehension strategies to understand what they read. *Reader-response learning theories* assert that readers create meaning as they read, and vary how they read depending on their purpose. *Sociolinguistic learning theories* state that thought and language are interrelated, and that social interaction is key in learning.

WHAT HAPPENS WHEN READING?

What is involved when reading? The simple answer is: becoming aware of text/reading material, sensing the material, decoding the symbols, processing the information, comprehending the information, evaluating the information, deciding what to do with the information, and acting on that decision.

Learning to read exemplifies myriad processes, starting with brain activity (Sousa, 2016). The visual aspect of reading begins with the eye sensing the orthographic components, such as printed characters, through the optic nerve, which carries nerve impulses through millions of nerve fibers to the visual cortex, located in the back of the occipital lobe. Then the information travels to the left fusiform gyrus, which stores the information as symbols. To process the visual information, a ventral pathway connects the visual cortex to the temporal lobe (located toward the front on the left side), which recognizes objects; a second, dorsal, pathway links to the upper back parietal lobe, which locates objects. Then the frontal lobe comes into play to govern

CODE: REWRITING THE STORY FOR GLOBAL LITERACY

CODE (Canadian Organization for Development through Education) has been "removing the barriers to quality education for the world's poorest and most marginalized children and youth for almost sixty years" (Library of Congress, 2017, p. 10). CODE started in a Toronto church basement as a donated-book program and now works with Canada's First Nation Inuit and Métis communities, and has even expanded to the Caribbean and eight African nations. Since 2019, Reading CODE has trained twenty-four thousand educators and reached a million students.

CODE's core literacy program is based on the idea that "for children to grow up into literate, independent, informed decision-makers who can think critically and successfully navigate the world around them, they need sustained access to relevant, quality reading materials and to benefit from skilled teachers." To implement this idea, CODE incorporated international experience and learning theory in its "comprehensive readership approach," or Reading CODE. While each county implements CODE in light of its own culture and language, Reading CODE takes a universal approach by:

- Valuing and building on prior experiences and knowledge, and encouraging children to explore, engage with, and reflect on the world around them.
- Developing and making available culturally relevant books and learning materials in the local language by local authors and publishers.
- Providing professional development for educators to ensure that they can use the materials effectively and can access locally developed educational materials for differential learning.
- Partnering with in-country teams to build capacity for sustained local publications and educator training (Library of Congress, 2017, p. 10).

language comprehension. The limbic system is also involved, responding to experience over time.

Although reading is typically associated with visual processing, phonological processing—the ability to manipulate the sounds of language—is also key. The sensory cortex takes in the ear's hearing. The temporal lobe decodes and discriminates sound. Broca's area of the frontal lobe governs language comprehension. The angular and supramarginal gyri link different parts of the brain to form words from sight and hearing. Fortunately, the oral and written language parts of the brain are close to each other. All of this happens in less than half a second.

The process of reading also improves the brain (Burns, Blaine, Prietula, & Rye, 2013). It heightens brain connectivity. It increases the central sulcus—the region governing primary sensory motor activity; reading action in a book actually leads to experiencing the sensation, which is called *grounded cognition*. Reading rewires the brain and creates nerve fibers that speed the transmission of nerve signals. Reading also increases the brain's capacity for memory because it gives more time for processing and imagining a story, unlike watching or listening to media. Because reading is a sequential activity, unlike looking at a painting, it expands attention span because it forces the brain to connect a sequence and make meaning of it; in that respect, reading on the internet tends to build short-term memory, but it can split one's attention.

WHAT SKILLS ARE INVOLVED IN LEARNING TO READ?

Reading Readiness

Even before individuals start to decode words, they need to be reading-ready with a set of conditions and skills that start even before birth. That entails brain development: the ability to sense the environment, store information, and process it. It requires motor skills such as eye-tracking ability, hand-eye coordination, distinguishing left from right, and bilateral integration (such as clapping). It requires cognitive and executive functions such as using working memory to remember words in sequence, having inhibitory control to minimize distractions, and thinking flexibly to interpret meaning accurately. It requires oral language skills, including understanding and using language to describe and deal with directions. It requires social skills such as joint (shared) attention and communicating information to others.

What can people do to help preschoolers improve their reading readiness? Here are some developmentally appropriate activities.

- Listen to sounds in the environment: in nature, words, stories, songs.
- Make sounds: model how sounds are made with the mouth.
- Sing songs and make up poems, especially ones that rhyme or have alliteration.
- Explain vocabulary.
- Play games such as "I Spy," especially if they involve wordplay or word patterns.
- Look at reading materials together: picture books, alphabet books, concept books, magazines, newspapers. Ask questions and converse about what is happening in stories; choose materials that interest the child.
- Identify sounds in words: beginning sounds and associated letters such as D: daddy, dog, dirt.
- Beat out syllables in words.
- Label children's drawings.
- Create shopping lists together and draw pictures beside the items; read items in the store.

- Ensure a nutritional diet, daily exercise, and adequate sleep. Check eyesight.

YAYASAN SULINAMA

Yayasan Sulinama (YS) is a nonprofit local development organization whose vision is to improve the lives of the people of Maluku and beyond in Indonesia through programs devoted to community development (social, economic, health), education, literacy, and language development. YS believes it can achieve this vision by equipping the community with the knowledge, skills, and attitudes needed for a successful life. (Library of Congress, 2017, p. 12)

YS has been working primarily with private preschools in central Maluku to help underserved low-income families who could not otherwise pay for early education. YA works to prepare these preschoolers cognitively and physically to enter primary education (Library of Congress, 2017, p. 12).

Fundamental Reading Skills

What characteristics define skilled readers? They can read long passages of text quickly and effortlessly. They engage with, and make meaning of, a variety of texts while adjusting their reading strategy to match the type of text and purpose. They share and self-regulate their reading. More basically, they value reading. People tend to become skilled readers through initial pleasant experiences with text and stories, much exposure to texts and stories, and a desire for more pleasurable experiences through hearing more stories and reading independently, practicing lots of listening and reading, gaining self-confidence as a reader, and wanting to do it more (Ross, McKechnie, & Rothbauer, 2006).

Several fundamental skills are needed in order to become a skilled reader (Hess, 2007; National Reading Panel, 2000):

- Phonological awareness: recognizing and working with sounds in spoken language
- Phonemic awareness: hearing and working with individual sounds in words (i.e., phonemes)
- Phonics: understanding the alphabetic or orthographic principle that a writing system represents the sounds of a spoken language
- Decoding: using visual, syntactic (sentence structure), and semantic (context) cues to make meaning from words and sentences
- Fluency: reading accurately at an appropriate rate, with suitable expression. Fluency is needed for comprehension and motivated reading.
- Vocabulary: understand the meaning of words

- Comprehension: making meaning of the text by drawing on their experiences, vocabulary, language structure, and reading strategies.

In terms of how the brain is involved, when it processes the same configuration of letters repeatedly, it starts to store them as a single unit of information. By chunking these letters (such as words), the brain uses less processing space so it can decode automatically and concentrate on comprehending ideas, as well as incorporating syntactic and semantic understanding (Sousa, 2016).

READING INSTRUCTION

Reading is a learned skill that takes place throughout life in many settings. While the underlying skills are universal, how people teach and gain these skills differs by personal, cultural, and environmental factors.

How Do People Acquire Reading Skills?

Every human has a basic desire to have their needs met. Children are especially dependent on others, and quickly learn to communicate their needs physically—by body language (paralanguage) and sound—with the expectation that someone will respond and meet their needs, be it food, safety, or comfort. Spoken language is the default first two-way communication channel; individuals who are deaf tend to use visual means to communicate, which is why parents are urged to use sign language as early as possible. In either case, natural language precedes written language. Mimicking and working with daily natural language lead organically to syntactic knowledge and skills of structuring sentences used by significant people who are nearby.

The link between first language and written language requires some deliberate action, although not necessarily formal education. For instance, by reading aloud to a child, the reader is modeling how print symbols are associated with language. As for directly linking spoken and written words, finger-tracking words while reading aloud provides a visual cue for the relationship between spoken and written words (prephonemic awareness). Visually linking sign language to written words works in a similar fashion, although it usually requires two people or a digital solution. At the other end of the scale, identifying individual letters or other orthographic characters and sounding them out demonstrate an aspect of phonics; shaping those letters adds a valuable kinesthetic dimension to the process. All these actions constitute reading-readiness actions.

More sophisticated reading skills may be subject-specific, such as chemistry lab reports or musical scores; specialized vocabulary and writing conventions must be learned. More advanced reading skills for diagnosing and addressing specific reading problems generally call for trained expertise, frequently supported by tested curricula. As many basic literacy projects have found, one does not necessarily have to pursue a college degree to support struggling readers. Instead, targeted training for specific populations can suffice, especially for one-to-one efforts (Culatta, Hall-Kenyon, & Black, 2013; Jacob, Armstrong, & Willard, 2015). The fact that a person cares enough to provide regular personalized reading coaching as long as needed helps establish a trusting relationship with the reader, facilitating an emotionally pleasant and successful reading experience.

General Effective Reading Instructional Practices

> ### VISUAL LANGUAGE AND VISUAL LEARNING (VL2)
>
> VL2 is a Science of Learning Center in the United States, funded by the National Science Foundation and Gallaudet University. VL2 researches the impact of visual processes, visual language, and visually based social experiences on language and literacy development in children, especially young deaf visual learners. Motion Light Lab (ML2), one of VL2's four hubs, is a space where digital technology enhances immersive learning experiences with creative literature. Motion Light Lab then draws on VL2 research to develop resources, such as VL2 Storybook Apps, and runs the VL2 Storybook Creator program (Lamolinara, 2018).

Some practices to help individuals gain reading literacy skills apply to most populations and environments. The following strategies are research-based and well-tested over time (Gambrell, Malloy, & Mazzoni, 2007; Gambrell & Marinek, 2019; Zemelman, Daniel, & Hyde, 2012). They target teachers—a term used very broadly here to encompass people who have responsibility to help others develop literacy skills.

- Create a high-quality, relevant, and varied print-rich environment that fosters literacy motivation.
- Ensure positive adult-child relationships.
- Incorporate several texts that build on learners' prior knowledge, expand vocabulary, and allow learners to choose texts.
- Model skillful reading, such as fluency in reading aloud, asking reflective questions, self-regulating, and talking about compelling texts.
- Broaden the definition of reading and literacy to include signs, graphs, comics, games, digital resources, multimedia, and so on.
- Teach purposeful, authentically meaningful reading.

- Provide both teacher- and student-led discussion of texts.
- Provide opportunities for independent reading.
- Balance meaning and skills.
- Balance whole language and skills-based approaches to reading.
- Leverage the reciprocity of reading and writing.
- Support and scaffold basic reading skills.
- Incorporate technology that links and extends ideas.
- Differentiate and personalize instruction using relevant assessments.
- Attend to the cognitive, emotional, and social aspects of literacy.

CONTEXTOS

Contextos provides literacy programs to schools, prisons and communities in El Salvador, Guatemala, and Honduras. Their Soy Lector (I am a reader) program trains teachers and other community members to facilitate reading and discussion by developing school libraries and providing targeted reading interventions. The Soy Autor (I am an author) program fosters critical literacy skills by supporting the writing of youth about their lives as impacted by violence. More than eight hundred memoirs have been published (Library of Congress, 2019).

DEVELOPMENTAL READING ISSUES

As people mature, they learn somewhat differently because of physical and mental changes as well as their accumulated prior experience and knowledge. Each stage in life offers unique opportunities to gain reading and more general literacy skills.

Early Childhood

By age 5, most children are able to develop conventional reading and writing skills, even taking socioeconomic status into account. The National Early Literacy Panel (2008) identified six research-based predictive variables of later literacy development:

1. Knowledge of the alphabet and sounds of letters or other orthographic characters
2. Rapid automatic naming of letters or digits
3. Rapid automatic naming of common objects of colors
4. Writing one's name
5. Phonological awareness
6. Phonological memory

Research increasingly emphasizes the importance of early childhood literacy activities (National Institute of Child Health and Human Development, 2006). Especially as the brain is more "plastic" before age 3, very early language-rich activities such as oral conversation, shared reading, and physically manipulating letter shapes all help the brain build and reinforce neuron connections. For instance, the act of exposing babies to two languages by 8 months sets the basis of fluency in both languages without an accent (Mustard, 2006). On the other hand, by 18 months, significant disparities in language processing and vocabulary are evident along socioeconomic lines—differences that can grow over time (Fernald, Marchman, & Weisleder, 2013). Other factors impacting children's literacy development are health, geography, gender, and social norms (Irwin, Siddiqi, & Hertzman, 2007). Therefore, positive nurturing and early literacy practices can help equalize foundations for children's life trajectory.

Just as important is the local environment. Optimally, the home and childcare center should contain a variety of textual materials, such as books, periodicals, cards, games, captioned TV, and online materials. Libraries offer a way to provide a changing variety of free reading materials; they also demonstrate a positive societal practice of responsible resource sharing. Writing materials—paper, pencils, crayons—should be available. Additionally, manipulatable toys and household items such as utensils and boxes are useful because they help children develop motor skills; these items can also be labeled as another way to link objects with the written word.

Children should also have regular opportunities to experience other environments, which can broaden their background knowledge and vocabulary: stores, libraries, parks, repair shops, and so on. Taking public transportation can be a valuable learning experience and an opportunity to engage with authentic textual information.

Part of the environment is social: physical and language interaction, emotional bonding and support, and shared everyday literacy activities such as shopping and cooking. Modeling functional literacy and leisure reading also gives concrete evidence of the benefits of reading. Shared literacy experiences can be part of healthy habits too, guided by caring adults—preparing healthy foods and reading just before bedtime to ensure proper sleep. More fundamentally, parents and guardians know their children better than anyone else, and so can tap into their youngsters' interests, needs, and capabilities better than anyone else in these literacy practices.

Family lap reading exemplifies how these components work together. Having quiet one-to-one time demonstrates an individual caring relationship, free from distraction. Choosing reading material that interests the child also shows caring. Reading aloud with adult and child looking at the text together reinforces joint attention skills. Furthermore, because the child can feel the sounds of reading as they reverberate in the body, the cuddling position evokes warm connections between reading and caregiving. Other good reading-readiness activities have already been mentioned.

STATE LIBRARY OF WESTERN AUSTRALIA

Yearly, Better Beginnings gives more than sixty thousand parents a new insight into reading with their children and shows them how to have fun reading to and teaching their children. Partnerships between child health nurses and schools enable every baby born in Western Australia and all kindergarten children to receive free picture books, and families get literacy information to foster shared reading and parental involvement. Libraries provide Baby Rhyme Time and Story Time programs, and Sing with Me reading packs provide parents with resources to use at home. (Library of Congress, 2017).

Although families constitute the first teachers, other informal educational experiences are valuable for preschoolers (Committee on Early Childhood Pedagogy, 2000; International Literacy Association, 2018). In these other settings, under the guidance of trained and caring professionals, youngsters can gain language and social competence with other adults and peers. Such settings can also stimulate and expand preschoolers' engagement with other developmentally appropriate literacy-related resources that might not be feasible at the home scale, such as collections of oversize books and puppets. High-quality preschool programs have low adult-child ratios to maximize teacher-child interactions and individualized support.

Such preschool programs typically include a literacy-based curriculum and structured time, both of which help youngsters become more school- and reading-ready. Typical activities that promote early literacy skills include story reading, wordplay, class conversations, identifying letters and words, prewriting, problem solving, imaginative drama, and playing "house" and other imitative life skills. High-quality programs also incorporate ongoing assessment and targeted interventions to help preschoolers have successful learning experiences. Such timely interventions are particularly impactful for disadvantaged youngsters. For instance, high-quality programs can help offset factors such as child neglect, parent illiteracy, and limited English-language proficiency (Currie, 2001) so that children can enter school more on a par with others.

The following digital resources offer useful strategies for early childhood literacy development.

International Literacy Association. (2019). *Digital resources in early childhood literacy development*. Newark, NJ: International Literacy Association. https://www.literacyworldwide.org/docs/default-source/where-we-stand/ila-digital-resources-early-childhood-literacy-development.pdf.

International Literacy Association. (2019). *Meeting the challenges of early literacy phonics instruction*. Newark, NJ: International Literacy Association. https://www .literacyworldwide.org/docs/default-source/where-we-stand/ila-meeting -challenges-early-literacy-phonics-instruction.pdf.

Learning Point Associates. (2005). *Reading: Birth to age 5*. Naperville, IL: North Central Regional Educational Laboratory. https://files.eric.ed.gov/fulltext/ ED489505.pdf.

National Institute of Child Health and Human Development, NIH, DHHS. (2006). *A child becomes a reader: Birth to preschool* (3rd ed.). Washington, DC: U.S. Government Printing Office. https://www.nichd.nih.gov/publications/ product/154.

Roskos, K., Christie, J., & Richgels, D. (2003). The essentials of early literacy instruction. *Young Children* (March), 1–8. http://www.providershelper.com/ uploads/3/0/7/3/30737125/14-the_essentials_of_early_literacy_instruction.pdf.

Zero to Three. *Early literacy*. https://www.zerotothree.org/early-learning/early-literacy.

Elementary-Age Children

Core reading practices are typically taught to elementary school children (middle childhood), as this period of human development offers an optimum window for learning such skills. Gerdes, Durden, and Poppe (2013) synthesized major developmental patterns for this age range. Elementary children can think abstractly and symbolically. They can plan and follow directions to achieve a goal. They can start to address complex problems based on concrete objects and events. They can understand the feelings of others. Older children want to master skills, both cognitively and physically, so this is a good time for them to hone advanced reading strategies and self-regulate their reading behaviors.

Recognizing this developmental level, the National Center on Improving Literacy (Reade & Sayko, 2017) identified the following reading stages:

- Early readers (typically ages 6 and 7): making words by linking speech sounds to letters; making sense of what they read
- Transitional readers (typically ages 7 and 8): using strategies to decode and read with understanding; reading like they talk
- Fluent readers (typically age 8 and older): reading independently and confidently; understanding longer, more difficult types of material.

In the United States, the *Common Core State Standards for English Language Arts* (National Governors Association, 2010) drives much of K–12 literacy instruction. The four main standards (p. 8) include:

- Reading: text complexity and growth of comprehension
- Writing: text types, responding to reading, and research
- Speaking and listening: flexible communication and collaboration
- Language: conventions, effective use, and vocabulary.

By grade 5 (typically ages 10 and 11), students should be able to (p. 10):

- Determine key ideas and supporting details, and make logical inferences.
- Analyze text structure and meanings, and assess how perspective and purpose shape textual content and style.
- Evaluate, compare, and integrate content.
- Read and comprehend literary and informational text independently.

Leveraging developmentally appropriate literacy development patterns, teachers should provide opportunities for children to explore reading materials before giving them specific reading tasks. In that respect, teachers should also allow trial and error so children can identify and learn from their mistakes, which can help them gain a more accurate understanding of ideas. Teachers should start with concrete examples, such as experiential learning, before generalizing concepts.

In examining how reading is taught in elementary education, Snow and Matthews (2016) asserted that primary grades tend to focus on "constrained" skills—that is, skills with a finite end, such as knowing letters of the alphabet and common spelling rules. Open-ended, unconstrained skills such as vocabulary and background knowledge cover much more ground and build on experience. The researchers contended that sophisticated teacher talk—verbal stimulation, interaction, and feedback—and content-rich reading experiences should counterbalance set curriculum packages.

The digital resources on the following page offer useful strategies for middle childhood literacy development.

READING PARTNERS

Reading Partners provides research-based individualized reading support to identified elementary students by working with underserved schools in fourteen regions in the United States. The students get weekly one-on-one tutoring in a dedicated "reading center" space by trained community volunteers who use the Reading Partners curriculum. To ensure that students achieve grade-level reading skill, Reading Partners monitors student progress and program quality. (Library of Congress, 2017).

Elementary school reading apps and websites. (2019). San Francisco, CA: Common Sense. https://www.commonsense.org/education/top-picks/elementary-school-reading-apps-and-websites.

Lane, H. (2014). Evidence-based reading instruction for grades K–5. Los Angeles, CA: CEEDAR Center. http://ceedar.education.ufl.edu/wp-content/uploads/2014/12/IC-12_FINAL_12-15-14.pdf.

Munger, K. (Ed.). (2017). *Steps to success: Crossing the bridge between literacy research and practice.* Geneseo, NY: SUNY. https://textbooks.opensuny.org/steps-to-success/.

Neuman, S., & Wright, T. (2014). The magic of words. *American Educator, 38*(2), 4–13. https://files.eric.ed.gov/fulltext/EJ1043526.pdf.

N'Namdi, K. (2005). *Guide to teaching reading at the primary school level.* Paris, France: UNESCO.

Peace Corps Office of Overseas Programming and Training and Support. (2015). *The building blocks of literacy: A literacy resource manual for Peace Corps volunteers.* Washington, DC: Peace Corps. https://files.eric.ed.gov/fulltext/ED591328.pdf

Reading resources. (2019). American Institutes for Research. http://www.sedl.org/reading/framework/.

Torgesen, J., Houston, D., Rissman, L., & Kosanovich, M. (2007). *Teaching all students to read in elementary school: A guide for principals.* Portsmouth, NH: RMC Research Corporation. http://www.fcrr.org/Interventions/pdf/Principals%20Guide-Elementary.pdf.

Adolescence

As children reach puberty, they experience rapid and significant physical, psychological, and cognitive changes, which impact their literacy development (Caskey & Anfara, 2014). As their bones grow faster than their muscles, they may have coordination problems. Their physical development also impacts their emotional and social development—they need to belong but also to be independent.

Adolescent brains change as well, restructuring neural circuitry and developing the prefrontal context, which manages executive functions such as reasoning and decision-making. As a result, adolescents hone their abstract thought processes, higher cognitive function, and metacognition. Part of this internal development also intensifies adolescents' curiosity and risk-taking behavior, sometimes without considering the long-term consequences. Adolescents can be very idealistic yet sarcastic, interested in social causes yet quixotic. Their moral development is typically the last part of their development to adulthood, so they may struggle with moral dilemmas as they are trying to wend their way through their social morass.

By the time adolescents reach their late teens, they have more realistic self-concepts and stabler personalities. They are likely to establish independent lives and seek romantic relationships. They will soon be shouldering adult responsibilities.

Knowing these changes, teachers should provide adolescents with authentic, meaningful literacy experiences that employ active learning. The learning environment should promote freedom to explore independently and collaboratively, taking intellectual risks while also offering a respectful safety net. Learners need to have increasing opportunities for choice, authority, self-assessment, and responsibility. Teachers can show the benefits of literacy by presenting adolescents with social issues to research and grapple with, thereby providing the chance for self-reflection and consideration of a decision's consequences.

These specific literacy skills are most appropriate for adolescents: reading for purpose, exploring different points of view, contextualizing information, analyzing how different media formats impact meaning, building domain and cross-domain knowledge, consolidating ideas, manipulating and applying information, collaborating, self-expression, and honing metacognition.

Struggling and aliterate adolescent readers merit special attention because interventions at this point can shortcut possible adult disappointments (Allington, 2013). While adolescents tend to do fewer recreational reading activities in general, at-risk teens are even less engaged than their reading peers for several reasons: lack of self-efficacy, apparent lack of interesting material, lack of autonomy, lack of personal relevance, and personal issues (Dwyer, 2014). To help these adolescents, reading experts are needed to diagnose and provide personalized interventions. Fortunately, by adolescence abstract reasoning is usually in place and teens can process information more efficiently, which can shorten time for honing basic reading skills. Motivation is an important first step and can include demonstrating the concrete, contextual benefits of reading, such as better health, more job options, and more responsible consumerism. Teachers then need to collaborate with those teens to provide authentic literacy tasks that leverage relevant reading material of interest to teens—and chosen by teens. Teachers can also leverage social needs by calling on the influence of competent peer readers and incorporating technologies such as social media for self-expression and communication. In the final analysis, teachers should build on teens' assets rather than their deficiencies to optimize their capacity for self-empowerment and self-fulfillment.

The following digital resources offer useful strategies for adolescent literacy development.

> **REACH**
>
> Reach Incorporated trains teenagers as reading tutors for elementary children, most of whom are urban African Americans. Besides the afterschool tutoring, the teens also have the opportunity to get leadership training during the summer and connect with an adult mentor for college admissions help. In the summer program, some teens write and publish books, which are donated to schools and other organizations. (Lamolinara, 2018).

Adlit. http://www.adlit.org/.

Association for Middle Level Education. https://www.amle.org/BrowsebyTopic/ LanguageArtsandLiteracy/tabid/103/Default.aspx.

International Reading Association. (2012). *Adolescent literacy*. Newark, NJ: International Reading Association. https://www.literacyworldwide.org/docs/ default-source/where-we-stand/adolescent-literacy-position-statement.pdf.

International Reading Association. (2019). *Engagement and adolescent literacy*. Newark, NJ: International Reading Association. https://literacyworldwide.org/docs/ default-source/where-we-stand/ila-engagement-and-adolescent-literacy.pdf.

Journal of Adolescent and Adult Literacy. https://ila.onlinelibrary.wiley.com/ journal/19362706.

Moje, E., & Tysvaer. (2010). *Adolescent literacy development in out-of-school time*. New York, NY: Carnegie Corporation of New York. https://www.carnegie.org/ media/filer_public/97/16/97164f61-a2c1-487c-b5fd-46a072a06c63/ccny_ report_2010_tta_moje.pdf.

National Council of Teachers of English. (2018). A call to action: What we know about adolescent literacy instruction. *Position Statements*. Urbana, IL: National Council of Teachers of English. https://www2.ncte.org/statement/adolescentliteracy/.

National Library. (2019). *Engaging teens with reading*. Wellington, NZ: National Library. https://natlib.govt.nz/schools/reading-engagement/strategies-to -engage-students-as-readers/engaging-teens-with-reading.

National Middle School Association. (2003). *This we believe: Successful schools for young adolescents: A position paper of the National Middle School Association*. Westerville, OH: National Middle School Association. http://www.amle.org/AboutAMLE/ ThisWeBelieve/tabid/121/Default.aspx.

The Meadows Center for Preventing Educational Risk. (2016). *10 key reading practices for all middle and high schools*. Austin, TX: The University of Texas at Austin. https://www.meadowscenter.org/files/resources/10Keys_Secondary_Web.pdf.

Young Adult Library Services Association. (2019). *Teen literacy*. Chicago, IL: American Library Association. https://literacy.ala.org/adolescent-literacy/.

Adults

Adults are more likely than minors to be illiterate, especially in developing countries where educational opportunities were less available in their youth or when economic constraints demanded that individuals seek work rather than education. In addition, females have been less likely to have access to education, or have been encouraged less to pursue it. Nevertheless, individuals can learn literacy skills even at an advanced age because the brain continues to change in response to behaviors. While communication between neurons and blood flow to the brain may decline, older people compensate with their experience-based knowledge, which provides context and linkages for learning. Rather, general health and physical limitations—such as hearing loss and lack of dexterity to handle reading materials—are probably the biggest barriers to literacy. On the other hand, such barriers may motivate elders more, and they may actually benefit more from literacy training than healthier peers (Dench & Regan, 2000).

Reading and general literacy skills remain, but lifelong language use and experiences can speed up interventions, just as they do with adolescents. Some factors to be considered in teaching adults is the reading material's semantic and syntactic complexity, its inference complexity, the amount of background knowledge needed, and textual features (Trawick 2017).

Because most adults who are engaged in learning reading and general literacy skills are motivated to do so, teachers should uncover that motivation and use it to design learning experiences, especially as adults want training to be practical and immediately applicable to their daily or economic life (Knowles, 2015). Thus, when working with adults to improve their literacy skills, teachers should leverage adults' experiences to help them link working vocabulary with the written word to solve problems rather than to memorize arbitrary content. For instance, if an adult wants to learn to read in order to pass a citizenship test, the teacher can use practice citizenship tests as a basis for reading materials and vocabulary building. Earning a GED (general education diploma) is another popular motivation, usually in order to get a job. In developing countries, adult literacy programs are becoming increasingly popular in the workplace in order to improve employee productivity. Depending on the local population density, teachers can provide classes for these kinds of goal-specific reading and literacy trainings, which then also offer opportunities to socialize—another important factor in adult education (Library of Congress, 2016).

The following digital resources offer useful strategies for adult literacy development.

Adult Literacy Tutors Association. (2011). *20 years of ALTA*. Port of Spain, Trinidad. ALTA. http://alta-tt.org/wp-content/uploads/2015/05/FAW-ALTA-20th-Anniversary-FINAL.pdf.

PROLITERACY

ProLiteracy has supported adult literacy globally since 2002, and almost a half century before that by its prior organizations Laubach Literacy International and Literacy Volunteers of America. Its core function is adult tutoring supported by evidence-based learning resources and high-interest publications. To that end, volunteer teachers get professional development and technical support. As of this writing, ProLiteracy works with partners in twenty-five countries, leads adult education research activities, and publishes materials in English and Spanish (Library of Congress, 2019).

American Library Association. (2019). *Adult literacy.* Chicago, IL: American Library Association. https://literacy.ala.org/adult-literacy/.

Center for the Study of Adult Literacy. (2011). *General adult literacy websites.* Atlanta, GE: Georgia State University. http://csal.gsu.edu/content/resources.

Dench, S., & Regan, J. (2000). *Learning in later life: Motivation and impact.* London, England: Department for Education and Employment. https://webarchive.nationalarchives.gov.uk/20130323040403/https://www.education.gov.uk/publications/eOrderingDownload/RB183.pdf.

Grotluschen, A. (2011). *Leo.—Level One study; Literacy of adults at the lower rungs of the ladder.* Hamburg, Germany: University of Hamburg. http://blogs.epb.uni-hamburg.de/leo/files/2011/12/leo-Press-brochure15-12-2011.pdf.

LINCS (Literacy Information and Communication System). https://lincs.ed.gov/.

NCAL (National Council for Adult Learning). http://www.ncalamerica.org/.

NCSALL (National Center for the Study of Adult Learning and Literacy). http://www.ncsall.net/.

Ohio Literacy Resource Center. http://literacy.kent.edu/Oasis/Pubs/0600.htm.

UNESCO Institute for Lifelong Learning. http://uil.unesco.org/literacy.

HABITS OF LITERACY

As explained above, sustainable literacy development is a lifelong endeavor. While some principles are universal, strategies to apply those principles vary by individual, age, culture, environment, and situation. Age is especially important because it reflects not only changes in the brain and other physical aspects of the body but also the accumulating experiences of each person. Therefore, the teacher should find out about each person's characteristics, assets, interests, and needs in order to optimize the conditions and efforts for literacy development.

It should also be mentioned that literacy requires practice. Just because persons learn how to read does not guarantee that they will continue to read. Without a steady diet of reading materials and the habit of reading, competency can decline. Therefore, communities should make sure that their members have access to rich, relevant collections of reading materials. Communities should also provide social opportunities to share and create recorded information to improve that community (Palani, 2012). Such efforts are discussed in later chapters.

TALES & TRAVEL MEMORIES

Tales & Travel Memories offers one-hour thematic literacy programs for older adults with dementia or Alzheimer's disease. Librarians and volunteers visit memory care facilities monthly with books and media about a destination in another part of the world, and engage participants cognitively and socially about the imaginary excursion. Pared-down Tales & Travel kits may also be checked out to individuals who want to provide this experience in a one-to-one setting (Library of Congress, 2017).

REFERENCES

Allington, R. L. (2013). What really matters when working with struggling readers. *The Reading Teacher, 66*(7), 520–530.

Burns, G., Blaine, K., Prietula, M. J., and Rye, B. (2013). Short- and long-term effects of a novel on connectivity in the brain. *Brain Connectivity, 3*(6), 590–600.

Caskey, M., & Anfara, V. (2014). *Developmental characteristics of young adolescents.* Westerville, OH: Association for Middle Level Education.

Committee on Early Childhood Pedagogy. (2000). *Eager to learn: Educating our preschoolers.* Washington, DC: National Academy Press.

Culatta, B., Hall-Kenyon, K., & Black, S. (2013). *Systematic and engaging early literacy: Instruction and intervention.* San Diego: Plural Publishing.

Currie, J. (2001). Early childhood education programs. *The Journal of Economic Perspectives, 15*(2), 213–238.

Dench, S., & Regan, J. (2000). *Learning in later life: Motivation and impact.* London, England: Department for Education and Employment.

Dwyer, J. (2014). Motivating the reluctant adolescent reader. Master's thesis, University of Central Missouri.

Fernald, A., Marchman, V. A., & Weisleder, A. (2013). SES differences in language processing skill and vocabulary are evident at 18 months. *Developmental Science, 16*, 234–248.

Gambrell, L., Malloy, J., & Mazzoni, S. (2007). *Best practices in literacy instruction*. New York: Guilford.

Gambrell, L., & Marinek, B. (2019). Reading motivation: What the research says. *LD Online*. http://www.ldonline.org/article/29624.

Gerdes, J., Durden, T., & Poppe, L. (2013). Brain development and learning in the primary years. *NebGuide*. http://extensionpublications.unl.edu/assets/pdf/g2198.pdf.

Hess, K. (2007). *Reading development & assessment of early literacy: A review of the literature*. Salt Lake City: Utah Department of Education.

International Literacy Association. (2018). *What effective pre-K literacy instruction looks like*. Newark, NJ: International Literacy Association.

Irwin, L. G., Siddiqi, A., & Hertzman, G. (2007). *Early child development: A powerful equalizer*. Vancouver, BC: Human Early Learning Partnership.

Jacob, R., Armstrong, C., & Willard, J. (2015). *Mobilizing volunteer tutors to improve student literacy: Implementation, impacts, and costs of the reading partners program*. New York, NY: MDRC.

Knowles, M. (2015). *The adult learner* (8th ed.). New York, NY: Routledge.

Lamolinara, G. (2018). *Library of Congress literacy awards 2018: Best practices*. Washington, DC: Library of Congress.

Library of Congress. (2019). *Library of Congress literacy awards 2019*. Washington, DC: Library of Congress.

Library of Congress. (2017). *Library of Congress literacy awards 2017*. Washington, DC: Library of Congress.

Library of Congress. (2016). *Library of Congress literacy awards 2016*. Washington, DC: Library of Congress.

Mustard, J. (2006). Experience-based brain development: Scientific underpinnings of the importance of early child development in a global world. *Paediatrics & Child Health, 11*(9), 571–572.

National Early Literacy Panel. (2008). *Developing early literacy*. Jessup, MD: National Institute for Literacy.

National Governors Association. (2010). *Common core state standards*. Washington, DC.

National Institute of Child Health and Human Development, NIH, DHHS. (2006). *A child becomes a reader: Birth to preschool* (3rd ed.). Washington, DC: U.S. Government Printing Office.

National Reading Panel. (2000). *Report of the National Reading Panel*. Washington, DC: National Institutes of Health.

Palani, K. K. (2012). Promoting reading habits and creating literate society. *Researchers World, 3*(2), 90–94.

Reade, A., & Sayko, S. (2017). *Learning about your child's reading development.* Washington, DC: U.S. Department of Education, Office of Elementary and Secondary Education, Office of Special Education Programs, National Center on Improving Literacy.

Ross, C., McKechnie, L., & Rothbauer, P. (2006). *Reading matters.* Westport, CT: Libraries Unlimited.

Snow, C. E., & Matthews, T. J. (2016). Reading and language in the early grades. *The Future of Children, 26*(2), 57–74.

Sousa, D. (2016). *How the brain learns* (5th ed.). Thousand Oaks, CA: Corwin Press.

Tompkins, G. (2018). *Literacy in the 21st century.* New York, NY: Pearson.

Trawick, A. (2017). *Using the PIAAC literacy framework to guide instruction: An introduction for adult educators.* Washington, DC: U.S. Department of Education.

Zemelman, S., Daniel, H., & Hyde, A. (2012). *Best practice: Bringing standards to life learning in America's schools* (2nd ed.). Portsmouth, NH: Heinemann.

Zull, J. (2004). Getting the brain in gear. *The NEA Higher Education Journal, 62*(1), 149–151.

2

Literacy Projects

L iteracy benefits the individual, the family, the community, and society at large. While some governments may be wary of a literate society because their citizens might access and use information that could oppose the rulers in power, even despots need to have their subjects functionally literate in order to obey commands and carry out necessary work.

The United Nations asserts that education is a universal human right and considers literacy to be an intrinsic part of the right to education. The United Nations' (2010) *2030 Agenda for Sustainable Development* reiterates the importance of a quality education, and explicitly addresses the need for females and marginalized people in vulnerable settings to get an equitable-quality education. In addition, the International Literacy Association specifically asserts that all children have the right to read. Rising literacy rates throughout the world give hope to global literacy. Formal basic education considers literacy as a core curriculum, be it at the national or local level.

DEFINITIONS AND CHARACTERISTICS
ABOUT LITERACY PROJECTS

What, then, constitutes a literacy project? This book defines a literacy project as a deliberate, concerted, and defined group effort to promote or increase

LITTLE FREE LIBRARY (LFL)

Little Free Library (LFL) is a community-based book-exchange program that fosters a reading culture. Volunteers build posted dollhouse-like boxes and stock them with free books to take and swap. Communities also identify high-need areas to install and stock these containers—for instance, LFL partnered with police to install these book exchanges near precincts. Little Free Library also supports reading advocacy, and their Whatcha Reading program encourages people to discuss their reading. This low-barrier, simple idea has spread to a hundred thousand book-sharing boxes in more than ninety countries (Davis, 2015).

literacy, with reading as the core skill. The typical project has a defined beginning and end, often with the intent that the target entity will integrate, institutionalize, and sustain the new literacy practices permanently. Technically, even one-time campaigns can spark permanent impact such as building a community library or enacting new literacy legislation. Likewise, one person might start a literacy project—for example, Todd Bol, who founded the Little Free Library. That project has been embraced by communities in ninety-one countries, and continues to expand even after the founder passed away; in other words, the heart is the community, not one individual.

Literacy projects can vary along several dimensions.

- Target audience: from newborns to elders, from illiterates to advanced second-language learners, from incarcerated teens to politicians, from single parents to intergenerational families, from preschool to graduate school, from policemen to health providers
- Lead group: educational institutions, libraries, museums, government agencies, religious institutions, professional organizations, workplaces, recreation centers, health providers, prisons, neighborhoods, publishers
- Geographic scope: from one site to a nation
- Time frame: fifteen minutes daily to one week each year; short-term and long-term training
- Funding source: donations, grants, foundations, government, event fees, service fees, product fees
- Physical access efforts: facilitating access to print, leveraging community resources, building community libraries, creating home and workplace libraries, publishing books in local languages, providing access in social/public areas and events, incorporating technology, providing access to readers with physical disabilities

- Intellectual access efforts: ensuring quality of instruction, selecting appropriate languages of reading materials and instruction, fostering early intervention and family engagement, diagnosing reading and digital skills, providing direct reading instruction, tutoring and mentoring, developing writing and other expression skills, basing professional development on research
- Reading promotion efforts: increasing awareness of the problem of illiteracy, working with government policymakers, creating a community of literacy, sharing reading in book clubs, offering literacy events and camps, increasing motivation to read and write, promoting literacy in service of social goals, promoting gender equity and maternal literacy, shared reading with people and dogs, storytelling, honoring traditional culture and mother tongues.

The overall outcomes of literacy projects include better and more reading, improved academics and careers, greater self-esteem and confidence, and community improvement.

This book further defines the scope of literacy projects to those that are community-based. Projects are planned and implemented by groups of a local geographic area or bound by a special interest or affiliation, and the community reaps the benefits. The Centers for Disease Control and Prevention defined community engagement as "the process of working collaboratively with and through groups of people affiliated by geographic proximity, special interest, or similar situations to address issues affecting the well-being of those people" (1997, p. 9). It is possible that a community would use a third-party product such as a mobile reader or even a national curriculum, but it is the local community that makes the decision to use those products, localizing or adjusting them to local needs and capacities. As well meaning as an outside group can be to help a community, there is a social and cultural barrier that is hard to overcome. Especially if an outside group comes and leaves, not living with the community long term, then the literacy project is also not likely to endure long term either.

It should be noted that a community is not generally a homogeneous group. For instance, most communities reflect a range of ages, ethnicities, interests, expertise, and perspectives (probably a good analogy is an extended family). Nevertheless, there is a sense of belonging to the community—a community identity that manifests itself as an insider feeling that distinguishes them from "others." Another aspect is the expectation that persons benefit from the community and contribute to it; its members are interdependent. While one could assert that everyone belongs to the global community, here a community is more likely characterized by its daily interactions and local governance, especially in terms of developing a literacy project.

Literacy projects not only impact the targeted audience, such as mothers who have had no formal education, but affect a myriad of other groups; for example, families, educational institutions, local businesses, health providers, and governmental entities are all impacted by a mother's illiteracy because the children are less likely to be reading-ready, family health may be threatened, income may be unstable, and civic participation may be less involved. Indeed, every person in a community may be a stakeholder. Typically, stakeholder influencers and decision-makers should participate in their community literacy project throughout its planning, implementation, and evaluation.

MOTHER CHILD EDUCATION FOUNDATION (AÇEV)

The Mother Child Education Foundation (AÇEV) began in Turkey as a means to train low-income mothers in school-readiness skills for their little children who had no access to preschool. Because many of those women were illiterate, AÇEV expanded their activities to include a functional adult literacy program (FALP), which uses a participatory research-based approach led by trained volunteer teachers. FALP now provides online learning materials and a literacy hotline, and its model has become the national standard for adult literacy education. AÇEV continues to focus on empowering women, and advocates for public policies that support literacy. (Davis, 2014).

WHAT IS THE LIBRARY OF CONGRESS'S ROLE?

The Library of Congress exemplifies the efforts of highly reputable institutions that promote literacy and publicly recognize impactful literacy projects. Other notable organizations that award literacy projects include, among others, UNESCO, the American Library Association, the International Literacy Association, and the National Coalition for Literacy. This section details the Library of Congress's Literacy Awards Program as a way to explain how such awards are determined and publicized. The program also provides a research basis for identifying key factors in impactful literacy efforts.

The Library of Congress serves as the research arm of the United States Congress. It also serves as the de facto national repository of recorded information published in the United States. Its mission is to "engage, inspire, and inform Congress and the American people with a universal and enduring source of knowledge and creativity" (Library of Congress, 2019).

The Library of Congress's central role is access to recorded information, but it is also interested in intellectual access to recorded information: literacy. In 2012 the Library of Congress was fortunate to have the attention of Carlyle Group cofounder David M. Rubenstein, whose generous seven-year donation has enabled the Library of Congress to have the opportunity to honor top literacy efforts accomplished by organizations. The awards also encourage innovative ways to address literacy issues and disseminate best practices. According to David Rubenstein, "Literacy spurs innovation and creativity. Literacy is one of the basic tools for making progress in life and can open doors to many joys and wonders. I am pleased to support the work of groups that help people become literate and successfully convince those who can read to read more" (Freeny, 2013, p. 13).

A $150,000 Rubenstein Award recognizes groundbreaking sustained record to advancing literacy. A $50,000 American Award recognizes a U.S. project developed and implemented within the last ten years that combats illiteracy or aliteracy. A $50,000 International Award recognizes literacy work done outside out the United States. The first awards were selected and given in 2013, and each year thereafter.

John Cole, director for the Library of Congress Center for the Book, served as the first chair of the Literacy Awards Program. Pamela Jackson chaired the Literacy Awards Program from fall 2016 to July 2107, at which time Becky Clark assumed the position. Then Dawn Sitzel assumed that position in 2018. The Librarian of Congress named a distinguished advisory board, representing several aspects of literacy. Advisors include authors, publishers, political figures, governmental and other nonprofit organization officers, professors, and librarians. Advisors represent the U.S., Singapore, and international entities.

David Rubenstein and John Cole developed the following selection criteria: innovation, research/best practices, replicability, measurable impact, and sustainability. Any of the factors might be relevant to a review of a program, but no single factor or set of factors is determinative; the criteria are meant to be inclusive rather than reductive. Applicants submit a project summary and letters of support; they can also list their website, which might provide more details. Over the years, the application expanded to include five statements explicitly addressing the selection criteria, the result of the advisory board's experiences in reviewing past applications. The change ensures that applicants can explain how they meet each criterion, and it eases the reviewing process.

Three members of the board serve as chairs to select each award, who select the semifinalists (seven to a dozen) for each award collaboratively. The rest of the board splits into the three award groups to recommend the finalists. The Librarian of Congress makes the final choices from the finalist list, which typically included three applicants per award. In addition, the advisory board earmarks up to two dozen programs that demonstrate best practices in some aspect of their work, such as improving the lives of unique populations (e.g., incarcerated youth or third-world garment workers), or using technological innovations (e.g., servers with public domain materials).

The Library of Congress publicizes the literacy awards program and its honorees in several ways: through the Library of Congress's website, http:// read.gov; the Library of Congress's annual National Book Festival; and the program's annual conference, which provides a venue for winners and best practices honorees to share their work and network with each other and local literacy expert attendees. The program has also cosponsored literacy events that focus on one aspect of literacy, such as health. Additionally, advisory board members have presented the program at events such as the American Library Association's Annual Conference and the World Library and Information Congress of the International Federation of Library Associations and Institutions. The underlying agenda is to share effective literacy efforts.

RESEARCH-BASED IMPACTFUL LITERACY PROJECTS

While literacy efforts have existed for centuries, a systematic effort to end illiteracy has taken hold since World War II. Research on the effectiveness of literacy projects is even more recent. Nevertheless, even in that relatively short time, much research has revealed effective practices for facilitating literacy. As communities consider developing mounting literacy projects, they should review the research literature to find out what practices have proven to be effective. Communities can then build their case and develop action plans that optimize the community's return on their investment.

Research has identified that the most significant factor in literacy is early childhood literacy effort based in the home (Barone & Mallette, 2013; Shanahan & Lonigan, 2013). Parents and guardians are a child's first teachers, combining language expertise and life-dependent motivation. They also set the basic environment for literacy learning. Does their home reflect a print-rich environment? Do parents and guardians value and model literacy? Do they proactively interact daily and meaningfully with their children through language? Do they introduce the written word through shared reading experiences, be it lap reading, following written directions, or reading signs in public places? One reason that early literacy practices are so important is that the brain is forming and pruning the neural connections by age 3. It should be noted that orality is the default way to communicate language; for children with hearing impairments, their first communicative language may be visual, such as sign language.

An extension to that early literacy philosophy is timely intervention (Foorman, Dombek, & Smith, 2016; Hess, 2007). The usual thought is that children should demonstrate reading fluency by age 9. Therefore, if teachers and other adults perceive a child struggling at that point, or even before, they should try to diagnose the problem so the child will not fall behind in their studies. It should be noted that the problem might have a physical basis, such as poor vision or hearing. Likewise, reading difficulties might reveal learning disabilities, dyslexia, or other special need.

The second major factor is convenient physical access to a wide variety of relevant reading materials from which the reader can choose, particularly those materials in local languages or reflect local cultures (Learning Point

Associates, 2010). It is impossible to become reading literate if never exposed to written language. The presence of written language reflects its value, so even if a family cannot afford to acquire print materials such as books and periodicals, they can borrow materials from a library or other community means of sharing reading materials. In short, all individuals, starting with preschoolers through the aged, should experience print in their daily lives (Evans, Kelley & Sikora, 2014).

In that respect, formal and informal educational institutions are obvious environments that contain printed resources. However, literacy experiences can occur anywhere: stores, post offices, religious centers, and so on (World Bank, 2012). Especially in places where people have to wait, reading materials can be provided, such as in hair salons and barbershops, laundromats, doctor offices, and transportation stations. In any case, the environment should be clean and provide comfortable seating, adequate lighting and heating, and quiet spaces so that the reading experience will be pleasant.

The notion of choice is key; it signals a sense of power and control, and it also surfaces the notion of personal responsibility, which is a sign of maturation (BookTrust, 2018). If the only reading material available is a prescribed textbook, then students have no ownership of that material; it is being foisted on them. Nor might that single textbook be at every person's reading level or interest them. Especially since initial experiences are so powerful, early successful choices in reading and the ensuring reading experiences thereafter reinforce the action and motivate individuals to replicate and build on that positive experience, which leads to literacy. Nor should reading be equated to schooling. Most libraries state that they provide materials for learning, recreation, and inspiration. Reading as a self-determined way to spend time benefits the body (such as releasing stress), the mind (such as building more neural connections and developing the imagination), and emotions (such as increasing empathy) (Clark & Rumbold, 2006). Choosing relevant and interesting materials and taking the time to enjoy them is very self-affirming. Furthermore, independent reading also correlates significantly with academic achievement (Cullinan, 2000; Krashen, 2004). This activity builds grammar, vocabulary, verbal fluency, writing fluency, and general knowledge.

The third major factor in literacy is intellectual access to literacy resources (Anderson, 1985; U.S. AID, 2016). Trained, competent, and caring teachers can unlock that intellectual gate. All teachers are, in fact, reading teachers, as reading and writing permeate the curriculum (Draper & Broomhead, 2010). Elementary teachers usually learn basic literacy development strategies, and secondary teachers usually learn how literacy plays out in their subject domain. As mentioned already, specific diagnosis and timely intervention can shortcut downward illiteracy spirals; specialized training is usually required at this deeper level of literacy training. Nevertheless, paraprofessionals such as parent volunteers can be trained in an explicit set of literacy skills, and they can then act as useful literacy support personnel (U.S. Department of

Education, 2001). It should also be mentioned that all educators need to keep current on literacy development as new methods are discovered.

Reading instruction itself has also been researched. Morrow and Gambrell (2011) synthesized research on best practices for comprehensive literacy instruction:

- Create a learning environment that facilitates literacy motivation, discussion, and collaboration.
- Provide high-quality literacy resources representing a variety of genres.
- Provide time for self-selected independent reading.
- Teach purposeful reading for authentic meaning-making.
- Incorporate tests that build on prior knowledge and that link concepts.
- Scaffold basic reading skills: phonics, vocabulary, fluency, comprehension.
- Incorporate technology to link and expand concepts.
- Use assessments to drive differentiated instruction.

While reading may be considered the interaction between the reader and the reading materials, the social aspect of literacy must be acknowledged—and should be leveraged (Trelease, 2013). No one really teaches oneself to read; another person (or at the least technology) reads to them, providing cues that link oral or visual language to the printed word (Duursma, Augustyn, & Zuckerman, 2008). Reading decoding and fluency improves with external feedback, usually from another person. A proven practice is shared reading or reciprocal teaching, which provides opportunities for learners to get peer feedback and support (Rosenshine & Meister, 1994). Technology can play a role in this feedback, such as comparing one's recording of reading out loud to a professional recording. However, technology does not provide a social-emotional motivation for engagement and improvement.

SMART: START MAKING A READER TODAY

Start Making a Reader Today (SMART) operates in 250 sites in Oregon to help primary school children attain grade-level reading ability. Schools and other community centers identify children who need reading support, recruit volunteers to tutor the children, and provide a tutoring space. Corporations and other partners provide books or the funding to purchase them so that each child can be given fourteen books to own. The program believes in sustained intervention; tutors meet with their students for half-hour sessions twice each week for seven months. Since its start in 1992, SMART has tallied over four million volunteer reading hours serving more than two hundred thousand students (Davis, 2014).

Up to this point, the research cited has focused on external factors for literacy. What about the reader? A teacher can only teach; the reader is the one who has to decide to learn. Indeed, motivation plays a significant role in literacy (Gambrell & Marinek, 2019; Wigfield & Guthrie, 2000). Usually internal motivation is more impactful than external motivation. If people do not see a purpose or benefit to reading, they are less likely to make the effort learn how to read. Therefore, knowing more about the target audience, including their wants and needs, helps motivate them. For instance, providing resources in the mother tongue or workplace tongue can make reading more relevant. Another motivating factor is the learners' confidence that they are likely to achieve the stated goal. A sense of control and ownership also motivates learners, such as being able to choose the reading material and learning activity. One type of motivating learning activity—or activity to show competence—is oral expression: reading aloud, storytelling based on reading, and acting based on a script or other reading material.

Self-expression raises up the important link between reading and writing, and the more general literacy aspect of "consuming" and production or generation. One of the motivating ways to learn to read is to have a teacher or other literate person write down an illiterate person's oral story (Morrow & Gambrell, 2011). Then together they read it aloud. This exercise not only graphically shows the link between reading and writing, but also hints at the original reason for writing: to record oral language for later recall. Thus, it is not surprising that reading and writing are often taught hand-in-hand (Graham & Hebert, 2010).

Another growing factor in literacy development that impacts access, motivation, instruction, and content is technology (Archer et al., 2014). Access to online digital resources is especially significant because it exponentially increases access to reading materials and learning aids. While much of online content remains textual, the added features of image and sound facilitate dual coding; learners have more cues in order to comprehend the content matter. The kinesthetic aspects of technology, such as keyboarding and touching a screen, also engage the learner physically. Online social media provides more opportunities to create, communicate, and share literacy products and experiences. Mobile devices play an increasingly important role as a platform for accessing and communicating content (West & Ei, 2014). In addition, in the process of incorporating technology, learners also gain digital literacy skills.

STORY SHARES

Story Shares is a nonprofit organization that uses the power of writing to support literacy. The Story Shares Hub provides a digital book-authoring tool and contains engaging reading created by its readers and other authors. The program focuses on struggling teen and young adult readers, and the Story Shares website enables teachers to track students' reading progress (Library of Congress, 2017).

SYNTHESIZING LITERACY FACTORS

All these factors together can combine to provide rich learning experiences that build into rigorous engaging programming (Farmer & Stricevic, 2011). Based on needs assessment, communities can identify target audiences and literacy goals. They can engage stakeholders in planning community-relevant literacy experiences that interest the target audience and that leverage community material and fiscal resources. They can identify content and instructional experts, and can ensure that sufficient personnel are available and trained in order to carry out the learning experiences.

Part of the planning and execution requires monitoring and assessment in order to improve the process and the outcomes, particularly literacy improvement (Hattie, 2015; Schutz & Hoffman, 2017). From baseline data about the target audience's literacy status to follow-up data after a program is completed, each step requires gathering and analyzing data in order to make decisions and act on them (IFLA, 2019). As processes unfold, corrections and modifications may be required for the planners to optimize the results. Such monitoring, assessment, and modifications are especially important because these literacy projects are accountable to the community in which they exist—and hopefully flourish and endure.

All these literacy project elements may be considered by the group planning these efforts. In terms of their organizational practices, several criteria indicate effective literacy programs (Clinical Translational Science Awards Consortium, 2011). One way to think about the organization is in terms of a system, analyzing its input and output (Melcher, 1976). The leader needs to coordinate those inputs and outputs, allocating resources to set the system into operation and then regulate it. A clear vision of the desired input with well-defined goals and objectives, as noted above, establishes the foundational input; this vision is based on the input of the community in terms of its members' literacy needs and the available capacity to meet those needs. This process also involves identifying key human resources, such as stakeholders, who serve as input and who can act to facilitate outcomes; the organizational leader needs to facilitate networks among the stakeholders in order to optimize communication, strengthen relationships, and leverage action on resource inputs. The defined aims need to be articulated well and communicated compellingly and frequently, which is an action based on the input. In terms of output, reached benchmarks and achievements also need to be widely communicated and celebrated. In either case, communication requires resources (e.g., printing, access to media outlets and telecommunications) and an effective communicator both in terms of written and oral language; the communicator *acts* on the input. Stakeholders can serve as effective communicators and can facilitate the dissemination of the communicated message. Other actors on resources are trained teachers and other staff, and have already been defined as essential inputs; these human resources may also need support to do their jobs, such as transportation, food, and childcare. There is an established need for resources, including curriculum and program content, as input must also include organizational resources, from supplies to facilities. Technology, including infrastructure and support, is another vital input, even if it is just a telephone number as a way to contact people; on the other hand, social media has become such an important communication channel that most organizations now need internet access and technical expertise. Organizations also need the stable input of sufficient fiscal resources—and fiscal agents—to enable the project to be implemented; indirect stakeholders such as local businesses can help most through financial input. These material and human inputs determine the capacity of the organization to achieve its output, or goals. In some cases, the organization may need to adjust its desired output—or it may seek additional resources (inputs) in order to actualize its original output vision. What is that output? It's people accessing reading materials at home, in public places, and online. It's people engaged in reading activities, alone and together. It's people expressing themselves through language: orally and in writing, on paper and online. The ultimate outcomes are literacy and the actions people take because of that literacy. It's people acting on what they read: making decisions that impact their own lives, their communities, their societies. As responsible and accountable community members, these organizations need to continuously monitor and self-regulate their efforts: their inputs, actions, outputs, and enduring outcomes to identify those factors that facilitate and impede the literacy vision.

Table 2.1 summarizes the organization's system for literacy efforts.

The Library of Congress (n.d.) Literacy Awards Program leadership developed the following list of programmatic criteria and associated descriptions.

- *Innovation*. Unique, original, creative, and forward-thinking approaches to literacy are considered when evaluating an organization's innovation. From implementing ideas no one else has tried to fresh approaches to community building and partnerships, innovation includes developing new and suitable solutions. Examples of innovation from previous applicants: leveraging emerging technology, teaching literacy to newlyweds, closed-captioned songs, and storefront literacy centers for teens.
- *Sustainability*. Organizations are evaluated for sustainability by examining several factors, including a predictable and strong budget, funding sources, stability of service, institutional support, and community participation. Typically, a self-sustaining initiative is not a onetime campaign, based on soft money or dependent on the leadership of one individual. Sustainable organizations often have several funding sources, as in these models: a baseline fund, such as from a national public library, supported by additional funding from partners for enhanced services; or several stable and

TABLE 2.1

Organizational System for Literacy Efforts

INPUT			
Human	**PROCESS/ THROUGHPUT**	**OUTPUT**	**OUTCOME**
Leader	Leads, coordinates, allocates resources	Vision, goals, objectives	Effective organization
Stakeholder	Brainstorms, networks, communicates, contributes resources	Ideas, personnel, facilities, fiscal contributions	Improved community
Communicator	Develops, records, and disseminates messages	Communicated messages	Community engagement
Teacher	Designs and delivers a curriculum and instruction	Curriculum and instruction	Improved community literacy
Staff member	Manages logistics, supports personnel	Documentation, operational resources, and programs	Effective organization, improved community literacy
Material	**ACTED ON**		
Literacy materials	Read	Comprehension, application	Improved community literacy
Organizational materials	Used	Documentation, application	Effective organization
Facilities	Used	Program space	Improved community literacy
Technology (e.g., hardware, software, infrastructure, internet)	Used	Access and use of information	Improved community literacy
Fiscal	Spent	Acquisition of materials, salaries	Improved community literacy, improved community

continuous funding sources, such as a foundation, sponsoring partners, and profits from training or publications.

- *Replicability*. Replicable initiatives help further the cause of literacy throughout the world. Organizations are evaluated for replicability by examining the ease and scalability of their model. With the details of the initiative and its guidelines, can another organization replicate the effort? Initiatives that succeed due to the influence of a small group of people, unique circumstances, or financial windfall are not easily replicable. Examples of replicable initiatives from previous applicants: train-the-trainer model, guides and tutorials, and building through existing structures such as health care.

- *Measurable results*. The impact of an organization is evaluated with measurable results in comparison with baseline data. While anecdotes are compelling, the impact should be in terms of the target group's improved reading competence. Ideally, this literacy improvement results in measurable outcomes such as employment and promotion, academic pursuit and success, improved family literacy, better health, and better consumer decisions. Measurements of individual improved literacy might include improvement in reading and writing scores, participation in reading and writing competitions, academic course grades, number of minutes reading, and reports of self-confidence as readers. Measurable impact may also include evidence such as enactment of literacy-related legislation, improved literacy curricula, publications by the target audience, new libraries to support increased literacy demands, more-literate employees, and the establishment of book clubs.

- *Evidence-based practice*. Relevance and legitimacy of an initiative are evaluated by examining its research and reliance on existing professional literature and applied practice. Organizations with thorough evidence-based practice cite research and clearly state how its recommendations have been consulted and applied to develop their initiative in specific ways. Some examples of demonstrated evidence-based practices are: research leading to the development of an initiative, and its methodology being used to demonstrate significant improvement; an initiative's impact being measured with the evaluation tools from research; and literacy researchers serving as consultants and external evaluators.

REFERENCES

Anderson, R. C. (1985). *Becoming a nation of readers: The report of the Commission on Reading*. Washington, DC: Government Printing Office.

Archer, K., Savage, R., Sanghera-Sidhu, S., Wood, E., Gottardo, A., & Chen, V. (2014). Examining the effectiveness of technology use in classrooms: A tertiary meta-analysis. *Computers & Education, 78*, 140–149.

Barone, D., & Mallette, M. (2013). *Best practices in early literacy instruction*. New York: Guilford.

BookTrust. (2018). *Choice changes everything*. Denver, CO: BookTrust.

Centers for Disease Control and Prevention. (1997). *Principles of community engagement*. Atlanta, GA: Centers for Disease Control and Prevention.

Clark, C., & Rumbold, K. (2006). *Reading for pleasure: A research overview*. London, UK: National Literacy Trust.

Clinical Translational Science Awards Consortium. (2011). *Principles of community engagement*. Washington, DC: Government Printing Office.

Cullinan, B. E. (2000). Independent reading and school achievement. *School Library Media Research, 3*(3). Retrieved from http://www.ala.org/aasl/sites/ala.org .aasl/files/content/aaslpubsandjournals/slr/vol3/SLMR_IndependentReading _V3.pdf.

Davis, J. (2015). *Library of Congress literacy awards 2015: Best practices*. Washington, DC: Library of Congress.

Davis, J. (2014). *Library of Congress literacy awards 2014: Best practices*. Washington, DC: Library of Congress.

Draper, R., & Broomhead, G. (Eds.). (2010). *(Re)imagining content-area literacy instruction*. New York, NY: Teachers College Press.

Duursma, E., Augustyn, M., & Zuckerman, B. (2008). Reading aloud to children: The evidence. *Archives of Disease in Childhood, 93*(7), 554–557.

Evans, M., Kelley, J., & Sikora, J. (2014). Scholarly culture and academic performance in 42 nations. *Social Forces, 92*(4), 1573–1605.

Farmer, L., & Stricevic, I. (2011). *Using research to promote literacy and reading in libraries*. The Hague, Netherlands: International Federation of Library Associations and Institutions.

Foorman, B., Dombek, J., & Smith, K. (2016). Seven elements important to successful implementation of early literacy intervention. *New Directions for Child and Adolescent Development, 154*, 49–65.

Freeny, M. (2013). *Library of Congress literacy awards 2013: Best practices*. Washington, DC: Library of Congress.

Gambrell, L., & Marinek, B. (2019). *Reading motivation: What the research says*. LD Online. http://www.ldonline.org/article/29624.

Graham, S., & Hebert, M. A. (2010). *Writing to read: Evidence for how writing can improve reading*. A Carnegie Corporation Time to Act report. Washington, DC: Alliance for Excellent Education.

Hattie, J. (2015). *What works best in education: The politics of collaborative expertise*. London, UK: Pearson.

Hess, K. (2007). *Reading development & assessment of early literacy: A review of the literature*. Salt Lake City: Utah Department of Education.

IFLA. Literacy and Literacy Section. (2019). *IFLA toolkit for developing national and reading strategies*. The Hague, Netherlands: International Federation of Library Associations and Institutions.

Krashen, S. (2004). *The power of reading: Insights from the research*. Santa Barbara, CA: ABC-CLIO.

Learning Point Associates. (2010). *Children's access to print materials and education-related outcomes*. Washington, DC: American Institutes for Research.

Library of Congress. (2019). *Enriching the library experience*. Washington, DC: Library of Congress. Retrieved from https://www.loc.gov/strategic-plan/.

Library of Congress. (2017). *Library of Congress literacy awards 2017*. Washington, DC: Library of Congress.

Library of Congress. (n.d.) *Library of Congress literacy awards: About the selection criteria*. http://read.gov/literacyawards/criteria.html.

Melcher, A. J. (1976). *Structure and process of organizations: A systems approach*. Englewood Cliffs, NJ: Prentice-Hall.

Morrow, L., & Gambrell, L. (2011). *Best practices in literacy instruction* (4th ed.). New York, NY: Guilford.

Rosenshine, B., & Meister, C. (1994). Reciprocal teaching: A review of the research. *Review of Educational Research, 64*(4), 479–530.

Schutz, K. M., & Hoffman, J. V. (2017). "I practice teaching": Transforming our professional identities as literacy teachers through action research. *The Reading Teacher, 71*(1), 7–12.

Shanahan, T., & Lonigan, C. (Eds.). (2013). *Early childhood literacy*. Baltimore, MD: Brookes.

Trelease, J. (2013). *The read-aloud handbook* (7th ed.). New York: Penguin Books.

U.S. AID. (2016). *Landscape report on early grade literacy*. Washington, DC: U.S. AID.

U.S. Department of Education. (2001). *Evidence that tutoring works*. Washington, DC: Government Printing Office.

West, M., & Ei, C. H. (2014). *Reading in the mobile era: A study of mobile reading in developing countries*. Paris, France: UNESCO.

Wigfield, A., & Guthrie, J. T. (2000). Engagement and motivation in reading. In M. Kamil (Eds.), *Handbook of Reading Research, 3* (pp. 403–422). New York: Routledge.

World Bank. (2012). *Learning for all*. Washington, DC: World Bank.

3

Literacy Partners

A case may be made that it takes a community to foster literacy in that literacy requires a pervasive and accessible text-rich environment; language and reading expertise; teaching skill and opportunities for learning; textual use and benefits; and belief in the value of literacy. All communities have needs relative to fostering and sustaining literacies. Because so many factors impact literacy, a variety of community resources and interdependent skill sets are necessary.

THE NATURE OF GROUPS

Most community-based literacy projects involve groups: to plan, implement, participate in, manage, and assess. In the context of partnerships, groups help scale up efforts and broaden their impact.

Groups may be defined as a number of individuals with similar characteristics and agreed-upon norms who associate with each other. Group membership can offer safety, friendship, status, and influence. Within a group, each member is treated as an individual; when interacting with another group, each group is typically considered as a single entity. Groups may serve a social function (such as a coffee klatch) or a task function (such as a political campaign), and the most effective groups entail both aspects.

Most groups have both formal structures and informal influencers. The formal side stabilizes processes, and the leader has legitimate power. The informal side can impact specific tasks and issues, and that leader may have expert or charismatic power. Other people in the group may have formal roles or titles such as secretary or treasurer. Likewise, group members also assume informal roles such as listener, encourager, pragmatist, synthesizer, distractor, harmonizer, problem solver, or evaluator. Understanding how groups work helps explain how decisions are reached, so that different people might be called on to facilitate certain actions.

Even outwardly stable groups, such as professional organizations, are dynamic within because of changes in leadership, membership, activities, resources, and interaction. Long-term partnerships may need to make adjustments as each of the entities morph over time. All groups evolve to some degree, experiencing their own life cycles.

- *Forming.* Groups start tentatively as they are creating new identities. They may be hopeful, unrealistic, or undecided. Short-term, small-scale activities with positive results can help people get acquainted and more comfortable with each other. People's personalities start to emerge.
- *Storming.* Groups form roles and expectations about acceptable behaviors. Individuals and the group as a whole may need to make adjustments. Conflicts may arise, and need to be resolved quickly and satisfactorily for the good of the group.
- *Norming.* By this time, the group has stabilized and has workable norms; the emphasis is on group maintenance. This stage can also lead to stagnation.
- *Performing.* Groups are efficient and productive. They have clear roles, monitor themselves, and tolerate deviations as long as their goals stay true.
- *Reforming.* If the group's goals and rationale for existing is accomplished, they may "sunset" their group. On the other hand, they may recommit to each other with renewed goals.

Just as groups are both stable and dynamic, so too can interactions between groups exhibit stable and dynamic characteristics. Hellriegel and Slocum (2010) identified six factors that influence interactions between groups. Addressing these factors head-on helps community groups work together more effectively.

- *Goals.* Mutually agreed-upon, clear goals help groups work together. Each group might have its own reasons and strategies to achieve the goal as long as they do not conflict with the other group. In fact, such a situation can broaden the impact of joint efforts.

- *Attitudinal sets.* Each group may have preconceived notions before it starts interacting with another group. As the groups work together, they may have to change their perceptions. Starting with a small, positive joint activity is a good way to develop trust and mitigate later possible conflicts.
- *Uncertainty absorption.* Groups have to negotiate shared control and power. Who has responsibility and authority for processes and decisions? What activities can be done independently of the other group? Usually documentation, finances, and publicity are central activities that need to be negotiated—early!
- *Task relations.* Tasks between groups may be independent, dependent, or interdependent. For instance, each group may create its own reading corner. A parent group might depend on an educational institution to train its tutors. Implementing a literacy program might be interdependent, as it needs groups to plan, manage logistic, provide expertise, and recruit participants.
- *Substitutability.* To what degree can people receive each other's resources and services? For instance, can people borrow books with different library cards? Can they get tutoring services from different agencies? For such substitutions to occur, the involved groups have to reach agreements about their interoperability, and need to make those agreements very clear to the community.
- *Resource sharing.* Groups need to carefully negotiate the sharing of material and human resources. For instance, a community library might also serve as the school library, under two governance structures—so hiring and remuneration decisions can be tricky. Likewise, collection development and payment decisions have to consider both audiences to ensure an appropriate balance of materials.

THE BASICS OF PARTNERSHIPS

The basic ingredients for partnerships consist of at least two entities working together toward a common goal, interacting socially, within a particular context. Each entity could consist of an individual, a group, or a system. Each entity has human and material resources that can contribute to developing and achieving the common goal, which then shape its role. Ideally, these entities and their resources complement each other. In public-private partnerships, the goal should have a societal purpose, such as community literacy, rather than a commercial one.

Partnerships are characterized as long-term, sustainable. and purposeful relationships. Not all community-based interactions consist of—or are required to be—partnerships. Montiel-Overall (2005) identifies several levels of interaction.

- Networking: informal social connections that can lead to joint efforts
- Coordination: formal relations between equal entities to manage processes
- Partnerships: working relationships of entities who share a common goal and agree on joint roles
- Cooperation: give-and-take working relations between entities that help each other achieve their own goals and see their part relative to the whole
- Collaboration: symbiotic relationships with shared goals, planning, implementation, and evaluation; goals could not be achieved by any one entity; tasks and social aspects both are present.

It should be noted that partnerships themselves can range from small projects with limited participation to decades-long, multipurpose projects with billions of participants. Likewise, partnership agreements can range from informal handshakes to legally binding contracts. Ideally, though, partnerships in literacy projects can result in greater credibility and legitimacy so that more people will participate and the community will benefit as a whole (McQuaid, 2000).

Even before partners are considered, those people with the initial idea for a community-based literacy project need to scope out the current situation. Table 3.1 illustrates the concept. The initial set of people should identify their own group's mission, resources, and services in order to make a strong case as a partner themselves—what they bring to the literacy table.

TABLE 3.1

Environmental Scan of a Library

	Internal Factors	External Factors
Strengths/Enhancing	Clear mission, trained staff, internet access	Family-oriented community, respected mayor
Weaknesses/Impeding	Old collection, few open hours	High school dropout rate, small-town budget
Neutral	Adequate facility	Adequate health care

Examining the external factors helps define needs and possible partners. While the number and type of potential partners may be large, choosing the most impactful partners is a vital first step. In the example above, the need appears to be an unskilled labor force, which might impact local business. Likewise, strong family values might help support more education and business ventures, and the mayor can influence community action. More information is required to make an informed decision, such as the local business situation; but even at this point, a case for a literacy project that focuses on economic literacy and job skills might meet that community's needs. Similarly, the mayor's office, school administration, library, and local business leadership would be likely partners for such literacy efforts.

In considering possible literacy partners, several questions should be asked, including:

- How might a partnership with group X benefit literacy?
- What benefits does literacy offer group X?
- What are ways to develop a relationship with this potential partner?

In other words, partnerships should be win-win propositions that the mutual goal can facilitate.

Partnerships require establishing and cultivating relationships, starting with getting to know one another. What are the partner's agenda and values? What resources and services do they have and need? Attend meetings and ask questions; observe the group's working climate and dynamics. Consider doing an activity with them—how comfortable is it interacting with them? Check their public relations—how are they regarded in the community as a separate entity and as a partner? Can they be trusted?

At this point, both entities can determine possible common goals, as well as the material resources and services that they can share and contribute. Does this partner bring something unique to the project, or can other groups serve as well—in other words, is this a good match? Expectations and roles need to be negotiated early on. A communication plan should also be established quickly. Relations take time and effort, but literacy projects place an added responsibility and possible stress, so the partners need to be passionate about the project and committed to carrying it out to the end.

Even when relationships are good, partnerships will be dynamic because each entity changes over time or under different circumstances. Even while planning the project, different skills might be needed than when implementing the plan, so different partners might dominate at each benchmark. Therefore, just as literacy projects require negotiating changing dynamics to sustain efforts, so too do partnerships—just as within-group behavior evolves. For these reasons, partnerships should ensure regular monitoring and adjustment, and they should recognize and celebrate successful effects, benchmarks, and achievements.

At the same time, partnerships have several drawbacks or can fail miserably (McQuaid, 2000). Unclear goals and strategies can lead to misunderstandings, lack of coordination, and conflict. Unequal power can cause coercion and resentment. If the umbrella organization has conflicting regulations and management requirements, partnerships may be difficult to coordinate. Partnerships can be costly, not only in terms of materials used but also in terms of time and labor costs; such costs can impact each partner's nonproject services, which could undermine their viability and reputation. Sometimes it seems that it is just easier for one group to do the work rather than spending the extra time and energy in developing and maintaining partnerships. The objectives of the literacy project and the input of stakeholders ultimately drive the decision about partnerships.

REPRESENTATIVE PARTNERS

Technically, any community group could be a literacy partner, but certain types of groups are most likely to serve as literacy partners because they are typical stakeholders in literacy efforts: they are involved in literacy efforts already or are significantly impacted by literacy. Some general practices apply to most partners, especially volunteers.

- Set and expect an inclusive welcoming and professional tone.
- Prepare a list of ways to get involved or contribute in order to help matching literacy tasks with people's skills, interests, and situations. Always make sure that there is a job to do before bringing on partners, especially volunteers.
- Interview people to determine their appropriateness for partnering. Explain the literacy program and its contest. Clarify expectations, procedures, training, and other requirements. State available resources, services, and supports.
- Document agreements and supporting information such as contacts and policies.
- Pilot-test new people by giving them short-term, concrete tasks and evaluating the outcome to determine if a good fit exists.
- Provide adequate training to ensure success from the start, and adjust responsibilities and authority according to people's growing expertise or changing situation.
- Provide opportunities for people to give feedback, cocreate, and improve the literacy project
- Be culturally sensitive and responsive. Honor their language, dress, and observances. If a person does not speak the dominant language of the literacy program, pair that person with someone who is bilingual so that both can participate appropriately.

The rest of the chapter describes the main kinds of partners for most community-based literacy projects.

Families

Parents and guardians (this book uses the term *family* inclusively to refer to both parents and other guardians) constitute children's first caregivers and teachers. Parents usually know their children better than anyone else, and they are typically more involved and more motivated to help their children than anyone else. Epstein et al. (2018) identified five significant levels of parent involvement, which can apply to literacy projects.

1. Family obligations: maintaining a healthy and supportive environment for learning, including literacy
2. Home education: monitoring literacy activities and communicating high expectations for literacy achievement
3. Involvement at school: as a literacy volunteer
4. Decision-making and advocacy: through governing bodies and associations
5. Community collaborations: as a literacy liaison within schools and other groups

Parents usually want the best for their children, but they might be reluctant to serve as a partner because of a lack of self-confidence in their own literacy, language differences, other personal and workplace commitments, or a general reluctance to join (perhaps out of fear if a recent immigrant, for instance). Here are some tips for supporting parent involvement as partners.

- Work through their other affiliations such as school-parent groups, religious institutions, youth-serving agencies.
- Provide examples of other parents' involvement, especially of families with similar demographics.
- For parents who need to stay home, suggest activities such as online work, preparing materials, or babysitting for other parents.
- To help with logistics, provide parents with transportation, equipment, or childcare.
- Mention that the partnership can lead to their own literacy growth and possible networking opportunities.
- Be clear about issues of privacy, confidentiality, safety, and options to withdraw from the partnership.
- Explain that often the best way to partner is to provide their own children with a safe, healthy, loving, supportive, and stable home environment.

Parenting education constitutes another way that parents can partner in literacy projects. Nowadays, more than ever, parenting is a complex and challenging job; at the same time, giving children a high-quality home environment

---

MOTHEREAD/FATHEREAD COLORADO (MFC)

Motheread/Fatheread Colorado (MFC) fosters parent/guardian involvement in their preschoolers' cognitive development through training by professionals and volunteers. These workers, who are themselves trained by MFC, use the program's literacy curriculum that includes children's books and adult narratives and poems to teach literacy-promoting skills for the whole family (Freeny, 2013).

---

has lasting repercussions. As parents gain literacy skills, they learn how to teach their children. In that respect, parenting education resembles teacher induction rather than passive reception of information. Even issues such as fiscal management and health practices may be couched as helping parents optimize the preconditions for reading readiness and academic success. In any case, parent education needs to build on parents' assets rather than taking a deficiency approach. Emphasizing that parents are a vital part of the community team to raise children to be literate, productive, and self-fulfilled adults should be the underlying philosophy of parenting education. By partnering with other parents and relevant stakeholders in literacy projects, parents broaden their community network and gain access to more resources and services that can enhance their family. In the process, parents may well have expertise that they can share with others, such as food preparation, storytelling, household management, handcrafts, games, outdoor activities, and creative discipline. The more that parents can cocreate and co-implement parenting education, the more the community will benefit.

Here are some basic resources to consult when considering families as literacy partners.

Every Child Ready to Read. http://everychildreadytoread.org/.

National Center for Families Learning. https://www.familieslearning.org/.

Project Appleseed. https://www.projectappleseed.org/activities.

Reach Out and Read. http://www.reachoutandread.org.

Sapin, C., Padak, N., & Baycich, D. (2008). *Family literacy resource notebook*. Kent, OH: Ohio Literacy Resource Center. http://literacy.kent.edu/Oasis/famlitnotebook/.

Zero to Three. https://www.zerotothree.org/.

Schools

Formal educational settings constitute the default site and means for teaching literacy competency. K–12 schools were established to provide such instruction in an efficient manner by trained teachers to groups of young people before they entered the workforce. The school setting also facilitates practicing literacy skills independently and collaboratively in subject matter contexts with peers who

PARENT-CHILD HOME PROGRAM (PCHP)

The Parent-Child Home Program (PCHP) focuses on school readiness for children with disadvantages. To that end, nationally trained site coordinators oversee well-prepared early literacy specialists from the community. Those specialists work twice a week for two years with families, modeling literacy activities; the preschoolers get a culturally relevant and developmentally appropriate book or educational toy. As they build a relationship with the family, the specialists also help parents enroll their children in high-quality early educational settings. The PCHP model has been replicated in fifteen U.S. states and six countries (Library of Congress, 2016).

are approximately at the same developmental stage. As such, schools serve as natural literacy partners for community-based literacy projects.

Depending on their size, schools can be complex systems, and each set of people can make up a partnership by themselves, depending on their function. For instance, administrators are key decision-makers and leaders, allocating material and human resources for literacy and other priorities. Support staff handle much of the school's logistics and documentation, providing the infrastructure to coordinate literacy and other educational efforts; technology specialists play an increasingly important role in such support, including ensuring that technology operates well for literacy purposes. Parent groups also provide support through volunteer work, donations, and governance; their daily care of children can motivate them to push for a strong literacy curriculum. Schools would not exist without students, so students can also serve as valuable partners, especially in terms of input about literacy resources and instruction. Additionally, adolescents can serve as literacy volunteers for children, and can help all ages with technologies that support literacy.

Among these groups, teachers represent the most obvious literacy partner. Most teachers are trained in literacy instructional methods—usually generic reading development methods in elementary schools and content-specific literacy practices in secondary schools. Many community-based literacy programs ask schoolteachers to train volunteers in specific literacy interventions such as phonics, writing support, and tutoring so that struggling readers can receive intense individualized attention. Teachers can also develop or localize a literacy curriculum and specific learning activities for others to implement.

The other obvious literacy partner is the school librarian, who provides collections of literacy materials professionally selected for the school community. Because school librarians work with all the students and adults across the curriculum, they know students' reading interests and needs, and teach them developmentally appropriate information and media literacy skills; school librarians also promote reading for enjoyment and help instill the habit of reading. School librarians can bring their deep knowledge of literacies,

KAZAKHSTAN READING ASSOCIATION (KAZRA)

The Kazakhstan Reading Association (KazRA) identified a need to update educational practices that emphasized rote learning by training teachers to incorporate critical thinking, problem solving, and collaboration. To that end, KazRA used the International Literacy Association's program, Reading and Writing for Critical Thinking. Besides direct training, teachers can access professional training manuals and participate in KazRA's conferences. KazRA's model has been adapted by several institutions in the country to improve educational practices (Davis, 2015).

research skills, high-interest cross-curricular materials, and instruction to the literacy project table. They can also serve as effective liaisons to both the school community and the librarianship community.

Most formal education groups support literacy projects as long as they do not undermine school efforts. Kindergarten and first-grade teachers greatly appreciate students who enter reading-ready and school-ready. Literacy programs that can focus on struggling readers or on language learners can be a great relief to teachers, especially those who have large classes of diverse students. Schools also welcome literacy supports provided by information education such as libraries and youth-serving agencies. The main drawback for schools to actively participate in literacy projects is largely lack of time (Duke & Block, 2012). In that respect, parent and student organizations within the school might serve as the best volunteers for literacy programs. On the other hand, in some areas of the world, teachers lack deep understanding of literacy development and best practices so they too might welcome targeted training that can improve their own classroom literacy instruction (Clary, Styslinger & Oglan, 2013). At the least, because schools work closely with a wide range of families, they can provide valuable input during literacy project planning and can publicize community-based literacy projects. Schools might also be able to lend the use of their facilities and material resources for literacy projects, which can significantly contribute to literacy project success. It should be noted that a school partner might consist of one group within a school; all the personnel at a school; the entire school community, including parents; a set of schools by level or geographic area; or an entire school district. The material and human

ESCUELA SANTO NIÑO JESÚS, FE Y ALEGRÍA

Escuela Santo Niño Jesús, Fe y Alegría began as a library created from a shipping container and developed into a public school that serves children in an underserved community encampment. The school focuses on literacy education and involves mothers as well. Books and lessons may be brought home, and mothers are taught how to share stories and promote literacy with their children (Davis, 2015).

> ## AMERICA SCORES
>
> America SCORES leverages the love of soccer to foster the love of reading; it also blends in service learning. American SCORES serves over three hundred high-need schools in twelve cities. This afterschool and summer program balances a literacy curriculum, poetry writing, and soccer, taught by the same teachers that the students have during the day. These teachers, who are trained by American SCORES staff, can then follow up with individualized reading instruction during regular school hours. In the process, the students learn team-building skills and participate in service-learning projects to improve their communities. As a result, students lead healthier, more engaged lives, and gain self-confidence to make a positive difference (Lamolinara, 2018).

resources that they bring to a literacy project can vary, sometimes scaling up efforts or providing specialized teams that would not be available at any one site. Therefore, literacy partners should be open to several possibilities.

Here are some basic resources to consult when considering schools as literacy partners.

Association for Middle Level Education. https://www.amle.org/BrowsebyTopic/LanguageArtsandLiteracy/tabid/103/Default.aspx.

International Literacy Association. https://www.literacyworldwide.org/.

K–12 Literacy Partners. https://k12literacypartners.com/.

Middleborough Public Schools District Literacy Action Plan. https://www.middleboro.k12.ma.us/cms/lib/MA01906409/Centricity/Domain/879/District%20Literacy%20Plans/Final%20District%20Lit%20Plan%202013.pdf.

National Council of Teachers of English. http://www2.ncte.org/.

National Literacy Project. http://nationalliteracyproject.org/.

National Literacy Trust. https://literacytrust.org.uk/.

Save the Children. (2018). *Supplemental literacy programs catch children up*. Fairfield, CT: Save the Children. https://www.savethechildren.org/content/dam/usa/reports/ed-cp/supplemental-literacy-programs-catch-children-up-2018.pdf.

Higher Education

Postsecondary institutions serve as an important research and education arm for literacy. As such, higher education makes a worthy literacy partner. While some postsecondary institutions have a narrow curricular scope, the majority of them are likely to offer literacy-related curricula because education constitutes a significant sector in the workforce. Higher education is also likely to support literacy projects because academic success depends on literate students.

As with other partners, postsecondary institutions need to see how partnering with literacy projects will benefit them and not overburden higher education. A couple of reasons may be compelling. Most faculty are expected to conduct research, and they sometimes have difficulty locating and recruiting research subjects; other partners in a literacy project may be able to enlist their personnel or target audience and supply possible matching donations for research grants. Such give-and-take between partners can strengthen the literacy project and its outcomes as well as inform faculty as they instruct. Higher education faculty may have developed literacy programs that need to be pilot-tested, which can drive or align with literacy project goals. As a counterexample, on their part, literacy project leaders may have developed their own strategies, which academic faculty as outsiders can evaluate in terms of effectiveness; indeed, higher education has increasingly been asked to serve as external program evaluators for literacy projects, from needs assessment instruments to program impact on target audiences. Several higher education institutions also maintain literacy centers, which include resources and services that can inform literacy projects (McGrath & Ervin, 2015).

Furthermore, field-based research can also include students as researchers, which can constitute as a positive high-impact practice. To that point, preservice teachers and librarians can learn valuable educational lessons by getting involved in literacy projects. For instance, preservice teachers can evaluate and modify literacy curricula and associated learning activities. Preservice teachers can also diagnose literacy problems and recommend or even implement targeted interventions for struggling readers. Preservice librarians can assess community resource collections and make recommendations for developing and using those collections. Indeed, such participation may be considered as service learning in which theory is tested in real-life situations to benefit the field, and then reflected back in coursework. In both cases, these kinds of partnerships can benefit both higher education and literacy projects.

As seen above, higher education and literacy projects both can benefit from partnering with each other. Nevertheless, challenges to such partnerships may occur. As with other partnerships, clear expectations and roles need to be agreed upon from the start. Time and site commitments by all entities need to be respected and negotiated. In the U.S., researchers need to obtain IRB (institutional research board) approval to conduct investigations, especially for human subjects and most certainly for minors. Such clearance can take months, particularly when several governance boards need to review and approve the intended procedures, including data collection instruments. Federal grants add another layer of accountability in that results and data need to be made available to the public, so literacy project partners need to be aware of such requirements. In that respect, university librarians can also help literacy projects in that they increasingly manage faculty research data sets via

ZÉ PEÃO SCHOOL PROGRAM (PEZP)

The Zé Peão School Program (PEZP) partners the Federal University of Paraíba (Brazil) with the construction workers' trade union to provide adult literacy education. The trade union realized that many of their workers have little or no formal education, yet they need literate employees in order to have a participatory and effective organization. To that end, one program, Literacy in the First Slab, focuses on workers with no functional literacy skills. The university trains facilitators to teach literacy, math, science, and social studies. Because many of the workers live on-site, they attend class four days a week for two hours nightly. To supplement the literacy training, a mobile library, a mobile learning workshop, and a digital media and art workshop are available to the workers (Library of Congress, 2016).

in-house research repositories. Student engagement in literacy projects may also encounter obstacles: getting university and literacy site clearance; having adequate transportation to work at the site; and scheduling time to fit in academic attendance, literacy attendance, other workplace requirements, and personal demands.

Other logistics can muddy the waters, such as joint-use libraries (Jordan, Lawrence, & Moran, 2018). While postsecondary and other libraries usually do not share facilities and collections, joint academic-school and joint academic-public libraries do exist. Careful policies and procedures need to be established relative to staffing, access, collection development, and services. In the best-case scenario, such joint-use libraries can facilitate cross-generational literacy efforts, provide cost-effective collections, expand access, and use staff more efficiently. When conflicts arise, though, such as staff or user abuse, corrective measures can be problematic. Despite these challenges, postsecondary institutions offer advantages as literacy partners, particularly for research and training. The benefits accrue on both sides. Dealing with the details can be challenging so a clear return on investment needs to be determined. However, the community at large can certainly improve as a result of such work.

Here are some basic resources to consult when considering higher education as literacy partners.

AmeriCorps Reading Partners. https://readingpartners.org/.

Georgia State University Center for the Study of Adult Literacy. http://csal.gsu.edu/content/homepage.

Illinois State University College of Education Mary and Jean Borg Center for Reading and Literacy. https://education.illinoisstate.edu/borg/.

Student Coalition for Action in Literacy Education. http://www.readwriteact.org.

University of Arkansas at Little Rock Center for Literacy. https://ualr.edu/literacy/description-2/.

University of Washington Department of English Community Literacy Program. https://english.washington.edu/community-literacy-program.

University of Wisconsin–Madison Cooperative Children's Book Center. https://ccbc.education.wisc.edu/.

Libraries

Libraries have already been mentioned as obvious literacy partners, given their function within educational institutions. Libraries also exist within other entities, such as businesses, hospitals, and government agencies. Even public librarians operate under the auspices of the community or other level of government.

All libraries deal with and promote literacy at some level, providing physical and intellectual access to information. In addition, the collections that they develop reflect the informational needs of their communities, thereby facilitating literacy engagement and improvement. In the U.S., most public libraries provide free access to most of their physical and digital collection, which serves as an information and literacy equalizer and social safety net. These core functions place librarians in a unique position to influence their organizations to support literacy projects. Librarians also network with each other, both in workplace settings and in professional organizations, which increases their potential as literacy partners. In addition, library users serve as attractive participants in literacy projects.

Libraries are likely to initiate literacy projects such as library card drives, summer reading programs, family literacy programs, community literacy events, oral literacy programs (e.g., storytelling, poetry slams), literacy-based clubs, language learning programs, literacy-based contests, tutoring services, literacy-based publications efforts, and information technology workshops. In these cases, their literacy partners are typically educational, generally nonprofit, governmental, or corporate. These partners may recruit audiences and volunteers, provide talent or expertise, donate money or material resources, or raise funds. In each case, the partners need to identify mutual goals, determine personnel and resources, negotiate roles and responsibilities, train and support each other, communicate regularly about processes and products, and assess to make needed modifications. As with schools, the main barriers for libraries as literacy partners exist because of competing demands, lack of available trained staff, inadequate or irrelevant collections, inadequate facilities, inconvenient access, and inadequate budgets. Government and corporate libraries may also have proprietary information or limited access to the public, which constrains their participation other than communication.

CALIFORNIA LIBRARY LITERACY SERVICES (CLLS)

California Library Literacy Services (CLLS) is a state-funded, statewide library literacy program run by local public library systems in partnership with communities and private donors. Library staff train volunteers and match them with adult learners to provide customized literacy coaching. Learners can also participate in leadership institutes to build their goal-setting, presentation, and networking skills. More than twenty thousand adults at five hundred sites learn to read and write each year (Davis, 2014).

Here are some basic resources to consult when considering libraries as literacy partners.

Center for the Book. http://www.read.gov.

International Federation of Library Associations and Institutions. (2018). *Guidelines for library services to children aged 0–18* (rev. ed.). The Hague: IFLA. https://www.ifla.org/publications/node/67343.

International Federation of Library Associations and Institutions Literacy and Reading Section. https://www.ifla.org/literacy-and-reading.

Libraries Taskforce. https://www.gov.uk/government/groups/libraries-taskforce.

New York State Library. (2017). *Summer reading at New York libraries*. Albany, NY: New York State Library. http://www.nysl.nysed.gov/libdev/summer/elmanual/index.html.

UNESCO Institute for Lifelong Learning. (2016). *Libraries and literacy: Using libraries to support national literacy efforts*. Hamburg, Germany: UNESCO Institute for Lifelong Learning. http://uil.unesco.org/literacy/libraries-and-literacy-using-libraries-support-national-literacy-efforts-uil-policy-brief-6.

Government

Public education and public libraries are typically supported by government at some level: community, regional, or national. Several other governmental agencies impact literacy efforts, such as public utilities (e.g., energy and telecommunications), transportation, and building regulators. Government agencies also depend on literacy to get work done—not only regarding their employees but also their citizens, in order to access and obey regulations, follow emergency procedures, practice healthy behaviors, participate civically, and so on.

Government agencies are valuable literacy partners because they typically have stable material and human resources; they have organizational and subject expertise; they allocate funds and other resources that can support

POLICE COOPERATION PROJECT (PCP)

The Police Cooperation Project (PCP) addressed the low literacy rate of the Afghan National Police by offering the officers an eighteen-month literacy curriculum, which results in a certificate that is equivalent to completing third grade. Besides gaining reading skills, the officers study math, health, religion, and police duties. The program has been so popular that a more advanced course was started to provide sixth-grade-level reading and literacy education, aligned with the national school curriculum and international literacy standards. Officers who complete this added course may be eligible for promotion or increased responsibility and pay. (Library of Congress, 2016).

literacy efforts; they set and implement policy that impacts literacy; and they can form coalitions to leverage expertise and resources to address literacy issues. When considering government agencies as literacy partners, groups need to make sure their goals align with and support government charges and priorities. For instance, literacy projects may focus on passing legislation that requires digital literacy preparation or guaranteeing more funding for library databases (both of which efforts were successful in California). One of the advantages of literacy partnerships is the governmental practice of outsourcing tasks, particularly at national and international levels, so literacy projects should be on the lookout for such opportunities. On the other hand, government agencies exist to carry out their mission, so asking them to participate in a literacy effort that is outside their scope of service is usually a nonstarter; lobbying efforts can sometimes override bureaucratic concerns. Furthermore, most government agencies have rules governing their participation in nongovernmental activities, which may constrain their participation even to the point that they cannot communicate about specific literacy efforts. It should also be noted that it is usually easier for literacy groups to think locally and involve community government agencies than agencies at a higher level.

Here are some basic resources to consult when considering governmental agencies as literacy partners.

Delaware Department of Education Literacy Plan. https://www.doe.k12.de.us/literacyplan.

Kentucky Literacy Plan. https://education.ky.gov/teachers/Documents/Kentucky%20State%20Literacy%20Plan.pdf.

Michigan's Action Plan for Literacy Excellence, 2017–2020. https://www.michigan.gov/documents/mde/MI_Action_Plan_Lit_Draft2_629757_7.pdf.

National Institutes of Child Health & Human Development. https://www.nichd.nih.gov/.

ProLiteracy. https://proliteracy.org/.

Room to Read. https://www.roomtoread.org/.

Save the Children. https://www.savethechildren.org/

UNESCO. *Literacy*. https://en.unesco.org/themes/literacy.

U.S. AID. https://www.usaid.gov/.

Nongovernmental Not-for-Profit Organizations

Nonprofit organizations are groups with similar interests whose existence is not dependent on making a financial profit. They may be professional organizations, such as the International Literacy Association (https://www.literacyworldwide.org/) or the International Federation of Library Associations and Institutions (http://www.ifla.org). They may also gather together people from different professions with similar interests, such as ProLiteracy (http://proliteracy.org), the National Literacy Project (http://nationalliteracyproject.org/), or the Global Alliance for Literacy (http://uil.unesco.org/literacy/global-alliance). Nonprofit organizations might also have literacy as just one aspect of their mission, as reflected in the American Academy of Pediatrics (https://www.aap.org) or Rotary International (https://www.rotary.org). They are typically mission-based and governed by volunteers. The U.S. has more than a million nonprofit organizations, and most of them have few paid staff members. Nevertheless, effective nonprofit organizations have a stable funding base and long-term practices and procedures.

Examining professional organizations reveals an inside look into nonprofit organizations and the factors that make them valuable literacy partners.

- Expertise and support on literacy issues, such as special education and language learning
- Professional development opportunities (e.g., meetings, conferences, events) to keep members and other current on literacy issues
- Grants, awards, and scholarship to support professional development and research
- A variety of communications methods such as journals, periodicals, websites, and social media
- Networking opportunities with the organization and other like-minded groups
- Policy statements and standards for issues such as intellectual freedom and access
- Lobbying presence for literacy legislation

Nonprofit organizations may well seek literacy partners to provide added funding, staffing, resources, facilities, complementary volunteers, and participants. On the other hand, nonprofit organizations might not want to serve

LOST BOYS REBUILDING SOUTH SUDAN

The primary project of Lost Boys Rebuilding South Sudan (LBRSS) is Literacy at the Well. This literacy project meets women where they spend appreciable time: at the communal wells. Project staff train local teachers and provide them with backpacks of waterproof instructional materials to use in teaching the well gatherers how to read. In a virtuous cycle, successful learners may be trained by the local teachers to serve in that capacity themselves. The project has expanded beyond the well environment to provide literacy education in community centers, markets, and prisons (Davis, 2014).

as literacy partners themselves if the literacy goals to not align with their own priorities, if they do not have the capacity to contribute significantly, and if the membership is not committed or available.

Here are some basic resources to consult when considering nongovernmental, not-for-profit agencies as literacy partners.

American Academy of Pediatrics. https://www.aap.org.

National Association for the Education of Young Children. https://www.naeyc.org/.

National Council for Adult Learning. http://www.ncalamerica.org.

ProLiteracy. https://proliteracy.org/.

Reading Is Fundamental. http://www.rif.org.

Save the Children. https://www.savethechildren.org/.

Zero to Three. https://www.zerotothree.org/.

For-Profit Groups

For-profit groups may be considered in two clusters: literacy-related commercial entities who provide literacy resources and services for profit, such as Pearson and the Literacy Company, and commercial businesses that are not directly associated with literacy but might support literacy as a way to support the community in general, such as Toyota and Dollar General.

The former type gladly wants to sell products to community groups. As careful consumers, literacy project planners should practice good comparative shopping habits: identifying and prioritizing the criteria used to review the product or service, locating reviews about the company and its offerings, contacting customers of the company to find out the quality of the company's offerings and their interaction. The literacy project planners should also ask for a demonstration of the product and time to pilot-test it themselves. The company's scale should also be considered. A national or international company may have enough customers that they can offer a stable, proven product and dependable service. On the other hand, a foreign company might

SIPAR

The Cambodian nonprofit organization Sipar promotes literacy by creating and stocking learning resource centers (LRCs) that meet the literacy needs of under-served populations. LRCs have been installed in hospitals and prisons located in rural areas and poor suburbs, for instance. One specific target group consists of garment workers who are generally young women who have not completed primary school; their lack of literacy significantly limits their life options. Establishing LRCs in six garment factories was just the start; the Cambodian Ministry of Education, Youth and Sport partnered with UNESCO and Sipar to offer literacy and computer classes at the factories during work hours. Factory volunteers were trained to conduct the classes and facilitate discussions about social issues; supporting learning materials, including a Khmer literacy app, were created by Sipar in collaboration with the Cambodian Women for Peace and Development organization. Besides these targeted materials, Sipar has addressed the need for books written in Khmer by publishing two million copies of 160 book titles (Library of Congress, 2016).

not have culturally appropriate material, such as basal readings about fish in Lake Michigan. In-country companies are more likely to have more knowledge about the literacy community and may even have local support staff; they are also more likely to have culture-specific content and the local and regional language. On the negative side, a smaller in-country company might not have a large market, so their prices might be higher or the quality of the product lower. Literacy project planners might be able to localize content, depending on the product—for example, they could incorporate local websites into a prefilled computer server of educational materials. As stated before, planners need to start with clear goals and objectives in order to decide which (if any) commercial products and services to purchase; the product should not drive the literacy project.

Commercial businesses, from neighborhood to international, may serve as literacy project partners as a way of giving back to the community. Businesses also support literacy because literacy results in more productive employees. Such generosity to literacy projects can also result in free positive publicity for a business, which can help their profit line. Some corporations establish foundation "wings" to coordinate charitable activities (Kwiecińska, 2015). In some countries, such as the U.S., the government may offer tax incentives for corporate donations in the form of material, grants, volunteer time, or cash. Businesses might provide printing services, meeting space, food, transportation, event prizes, or coupons. In terms of services, businesses can provide expertise such as logistics, accounting, and marketing. Businesses can also expand networking opportunities. However, support could be as simple as allowing a flyer to be posted in the store window. Sometimes literacy projects might focus on workplace literacy—either basic reading skills or job-specific literacy. In those cases, literacy projects are usually true partnerships: where the company provides the space, the target audience, and the specific need; literacy experts provide the literacy materials and the training. Companies often find that such workplace literacy improves productivity, product quality, and the quality of life for their employees.

One specific type of commercial entity can play a unique partner role in community literacy projects: media outlets. Newspapers, radios, and television stations need content for their communications channels. In the U.S., broadcast stations are required to provide free advertising—usually in the form of a public service announcement—for nonprofit groups or projects. Literacy certainly fits the bill as a positive, noteworthy endeavor. These media outlets are usually willing to work with literacy groups to craft the message for optimum impact. For their part, literacy communicators need to be able to tell a compelling story and get permission from the people involved to be recorded or documented publicly. Just as important, literacy projects should build on existing relationships with the media in which literacy stakeholders inform media about ongoing work as well as relay messages to their own community constituents (Ting Lee & Hemant Desai, 2014).

Here are some basic resources to consult when considering media outlets as literacy partners.

American Library Association. (n.d.). *Media relations handbook for libraries.* Chicago, IL: American Library Association. http://www.ala.org/advocacy/sites/ala.org .advocacy/files/content/ALA-Media-Relations-Handbook.pdf.

Howard, C. M. (2004). Working with reporters: Mastering the fundamentals to build long-term relationships. *Public Relations Quarterly, 49*(1), 36–39. https://search .proquest.com/docview/222400094?pq-origsite=gscholar.

Litwin, M. (2003). *Public relations and the electronic media.* http://www.larrylitwin .com/handouts/13%20-%20PR%20and%20Elec.%20Media.pdf.

Media Research & Action Project. https://www.mrap.info/.

Probably the most important aspects of commercial partnerships are mutual benefit and authentic relationships. Some businesses, especially at the local level, may be asked by many groups for some kind of donation, with no promise of benefits in turn. Companies need to see a good return on their investment. And literacy groups need to make sure that business partnerships do not come with "strings attached," such as branded websites or exclusionary contracts, which can compromise a literacy project's integrity and mission (Young, 2002). Another bad result happens when several people in the same literacy project ask for donations; literacy projects need to list the benefits to businesses ahead of time, and one person should coordinate local "asks." Ideally, literacy groups will come to the project with existing business relationships in hand so they can use an asset-based approach to planning and implementation. As with other partnerships, working with businesses requires articulated agreed-upon goals and objectives, clear expectations and roles, and sensitivity to commitments of time and effort (Laasonen, Fougère, & Kourula, 2012).

NAL'IBALI

Nal'ibali—"here's the story" in the isiXhosa language—is a national reading-promotion campaign that capitalizes on the power of the mother tongue. Nal'ibali creates bilingual newspaper story supplements in eight South African languages and produces radio shows of children's stories in the country's eleven official languages. In addition, Nal'ibali has launched four mobile libraries to expand access to children's books. Four thousand reading clubs facilitated by volunteers leverage these media stories to motivate children to read and develop a reading culture (Library of Congress, 2019).

REFERENCES

Clary, D., Styslinger, M., & Oglan, V. (2013). Literacy learning communities in partnership. *School-University Partnerships, 5*(1), 28–39.

Davis, J. (2015). *Library of Congress literacy awards 2015: Best practices.* Washington, DC: Library of Congress.

Davis, J. (2014). *Library of Congress literacy awards 2014: Best practices.* Washington, DC: Library of Congress.

Duke, N., & Block, M. (2012). Improving reading in the primary grades. *The Future of Children, 22*(2), 55–72.

Epstein, J., et al. (2018). *School, family, and community partnerships: Your handbook for action* (4th ed.). Thousand Oaks, CA: Corwin Press.

Freeny, M. (2013). *Library of Congress literacy awards 2013: Best practices.* Washington, DC: Library of Congress.

Hellriegel, D., & Slocum, J. (2010). *Organizational behavior* (13th ed.). Boston, MA: Cengage.

Jordan, C., Lawrence, V., & Moran, C. (2018). Experience from the field: Programming in a joint-use partnership library. *Reference Librarian, 59*(3), 134–145.

Kwiecińska, M. (2015). Corporate foundation's relationship with the founding company and its role in image building and corporate community involvement programmes. *Argumenta Oeconomica, 35*(2), 169–184.

Laasonen, S., Fougère, M., & Kourula, A. (2012). Dominant articulations in academic business and society discourse on NGO–business relations: A critical assessment. *Journal of Business Ethics, 109*(4), 521–545.

Lamolinara, G. (2018). *Library of Congress literacy awards 2018*. Washington, DC: Library of Congress.

Library of Congress. (2019). *Library of Congress literacy awards 2019*. Washington, DC: Library of Congress.

Library of Congress. (2016). *Library of Congress literacy awards 2016*. Washington, DC: Library of Congress.

McGrath, K., & Erwin, R. (2015). University-based literacy center: Benefits for the college and the community. *AILACTE Journal, 12*(1), 93–117.

McQuaid, R. (2000). The theory of partnership: Why have partnerships? In *Public-private partnerships* (pp. 27–53). New York, NY: Routledge.

Montiel-Overall, P. (2005). A theoretical understanding of TLC. *School Libraries Worldwide, 11*(2), 24–48.

Ting Lee, S., & Hemant Desai, M. (2014). Dialogic communication and media relations in non-governmental organizations. *Journal of Communication Management, 18*(1), 80–100.

Young, D. R. (2002). The influence of business on nonprofit organizations and the complexity of nonprofit accountability: Looking inside as well as outside. *The American Review of Public Administration, 32*(1), 3–19.

4

Literacy Issues

Fundamentally, literacy involves an individual interacting with recorded information within an environment. The process of becoming literate involves at least one other person within that scenario to help the individual intellectually access that information. The recorded information and both individuals need to understand and use the same language via the same senses. These are the basic preconditions. Even at this level, it is easy to imagine those preconditions not being met: no physical access to recorded information; no available second person with literacy expertise who helps; language differences; different sensory limitations; environmental constraints or distractions. This chapter discusses several literacy issues and ways to address them.

PHYSIOLOGICAL FACTORS

Chapter 1 discussed how individuals learn, starting with the brain. Sensory development—especially hearing—impacts perception and processing of language. Physical coordination development is needed to express language. Motor development is needed to coordinate bodily motions to physically access and handle information objects such as printed materials and technological devices. Chemicals such as hormones stimulate emotions and activity, which can impact curiosity, attention span, empathy, and other behaviors that facilitate and impede literacy.

If any of these physiological factors are delayed or dysfunctional, literacy development is impacted. Health providers understand the importance of human development benchmarks in diagnosing and addressing significant delays or issues—for example, some ophthalmologists provide free infant eye checkups in order to prevent later eye troubles. Increasingly, health providers recognize the link between human development and literacy. For example, the national Reach Out and Read literacy program for children up to age five is delivered by pediatricians and other health providers who provide books and prescribe reading aloud to encourage parent-child interaction in order to stimulate early brain development.

For these reasons, parents and other caregivers such as daycare personnel should check children's hearing and eyesight regularly in order to make timely interventions. They should also help children meet developmental milestones through language interaction, play and other physical activity, intellectual stimulation, and emotional self-regulation. Such actions by parents and other caregivers can constitute a vital part of literacy projects such as family literacy or daycare-focused early childhood reading-readiness programs. Increasingly, libraries are incorporating sensory rooms to help children with autism spectrum disorders have a more satisfying storyhour and other literacy experiences.

While most of our discussion has focused on early interventions, keep in mind physiological differences and challenges can take place at any age. For instance, disease and aging can impact bodily functions. Assistive technologies, such as customizable text and devices, can provide accommodations to help with handling materials.

RESOURCES FOR THE BLIND INC. (RBI)

Resources for the Blind Inc. (RBI) is a nonprofit Christian organization focused since 1988 on serving people with visual impairment in the Philippines through education and support. For instance, in partnership with the Philippines Department of Education, RBI has helped children with visual impairment achieve success in inclusive classrooms. RBI assesses children's vision, produces accessible reading materials, and trains teachers and parents to support these children effectively using a holistic approach (Lamolinara, 2018, p. 22).

PSYCHOLOGICAL FACTORS

Psychological factors impact literacy development as much as physiological factors do. By attending to these factors, literacy projects can be more effective. From their extensive literature review, Habibian et al. (2105) identified key psychological factors in the process of reading.

- *Attitude.* A person's feeling based on their reading experience impacts their attitude, motivation, and interest in reading in the future. That attitude also relates to their inclination to learn in general. If individuals have a positive predisposition toward reading, they are more likely to be successful readers.
- *Self-efficacy.* A person's self-belief about their potential to deal with personal challenges, to be knowledgeable, or to carry out an assigned task contributes to their self-efficacy. To successfully manage academic tasks requires self-efficacy, largely because such self-belief impacts a person's choice of activities to engage in, the amount of effort and commitment given to that activity, and the degree of achievement in that activity. Self-efficacy also correlates significantly with a sense of control. It should be noted that self-efficiency refers to specific tasks; it is not a generalized attitude. In terms of literacy, highly efficacious persons tend to read extensively and comprehend what they read, so literacy projects should help learners gain a sense of self-efficacy.
- *Anxiety.* Language performance is inversely related to anxiety, and many students feel anxious in language classes because of teaching style, public speaking, social image, competition, and testing. Anxiety also affects reading comprehension; students with low anxiety used background knowledge strategies and global strategies such as predicting, skimming for main ideas, and summarizing. In contrast, anxious students used local strategies such as dictionary use and grammar analysis. Literacy projects need to help learners lower their anxiety by stating clear expectations and beginning with low-stakes activities that help students take intellectual risks and use metacognitive skills. Letting learners record (and re-record) their oral performance instead of speaking in public is another way to lower anxiety.
- *Interest.* A person's reading comprehension, vocabulary retention, and recall correlate positively with the person being interested in the content or subject matter of the reading material. Less-skilled readers also improve their performance if they are interested in the text topic. Therefore, literacy projects should discover what interests their target audience and build on those interests. One approach to grouping readers is by topical interest rather than reading skill level.
- *Motivation.* It is not surprising that motivation impacts how people learn and how well they perform. Reading takes effort, so a person needs to be motivated to think that the outcome is worth the work. Thus, motivation is linked to values, which also shape self-identity. That motivation is also more impactful if formed internally rather than externally rewarded. Literacy

project planners should therefore find out what motivates their target audience or at least demonstrate the value of literacy and help learners internalize that value. Gambrell (1996) identified several practices for students that increase reading motivation, which can be used in literacy projects: print-rich environments, opportunities to become familiar with lots of books, self-selection of materials, opportunities to read in various settings, teacher enthusiasm about reading, parental support, social interactions about books, and reading incentives such as books. Similarly, Schutte and Malouff (2007) found four dimensions of reading that motivate adults: reading linked to self-identity, reading efficacy, reading for recognition, and reading that contributes to success in other areas of life.

UNITED THROUGH READING

United through Reading helps active U.S. military personnel stay involved in their children's literacy development through the filming of reading storybooks and distributing the recordings to their families. Research indicates that reading aloud to children improves their literacy skills. To carry out this effort, more than five hundred volunteers in USO centers and on naval ships help military personnel choose an appropriate children's book. Then the volunteers show how to read stories aloud engagingly. The military parent's read-aloud session is recorded and then sent to the family, along with a copy of the book. At home, children can watch the recording repeatedly and feel more connected to their deployed parent (Davis, 2015).

SOCIAL AND COMMUNITY FACTORS

Literacy development involves a social element—in providing literacy materials and environments, in teaching literacy skills, and in sharing literacy experiences. Those social factors range in scope from immediate family to the neighborhood, community, region, nation, and world.

Familial factors have already been detailed. Literacy begins with the family: providing a loving, safe, stimulating learning environment; interacting physically, cognitively, and psychologically with children daily in positive, authentic, language-rich ways; and guiding them in their human, and more specifically, literacy development. Families model literacy in their own actions and values, setting the stage for their children's literacy attitudes and behaviors. Whenever possible, early childhood literacy projects should include families. A family, by the way, can include extended members who may be far away but can be contacted through telecommunications, including the internet, and who offer additional caring, language-based interaction.

The neighborhood impacts literacy development similarly to the family by the extent to which it provides a safe, stimulating learning environment. What public spaces and services are available within walking distance? Are there nearby schools, literacy-friendly stores, newsstands or bookstores, libraries, other cultural venues such as theaters or museums, religious institutions, health agencies, play areas or centers, open spaces? Most of these places have signs or other literacy materials to read, and they are venues for language-based interaction. Children usually make their first contact with peers within the neighborhood, which can lead to entering other home environments with their own literacy presence or lack thereof. Neighborhood literacy activities can be impactful because participants can get daily feedback.

Communities are the main focus for most literacy projects for several reasons. They provide a sufficient number of resources and services to sustain an impactful literacy project, a broad fiscal base, a network of educational institutions, likely available literacy expertise, likely available leadership expertise, available service and volunteer groups to participate in literacy efforts, a large enough and diverse population with stakeholders to plan and implement literacy projects, regular communication among community members, possibly an established transportation system, local governance and supporting agencies, and the sense of an interdependent community identity. Communities also provide a variety of venues to observe and practice literacy behaviors.

Ultimately, reading and other literacies should be viewed as a normal part of community life. The critical question remains: Is the community a literate environment? Does it value and model literacy? People routinely hide their own illiteracy, using workarounds to overcome literacy barriers, such as asking other people to read for them because they forgot their glasses. People often do not realize the extent of illiteracy within their community, which literacy project planners need to uncover in their initial needs assessment. That first audit can then be examined in terms of the consequences of illiteracy on the community, such as fewer job options, health risks, more crime, and less civic engagement. Another way to frame the need for literacy is to envision the benefits of a more literate community. From that vision arises possible literacy goals and strategies, based on the available community resources and services. A community-wide awareness, commitment, and coordinated action can then make a real impact on literacy and community improvement. Nashville Public Library's (2013) Blueprint for Early Childhood Success is just one such community-based literacy plan.

CULTURAL FACTORS

Cultures are well-defined, sustained groups of people with common norms, expectations, and values, which can be distinguished from other culture groups. UNESCO (2002) defines culture as "the set of distinctive spiritual,

LEVERAGING COMMUNITY RESOURCES

Involvement and engagement of the local community in order to leverage its resources contribute immeasurably to the success of literacy initiatives, as shown by the examples below of Library of Congress applicants.

In the United States, community engagement is exemplified by the Queens (NY) Library Literacy Zone Welcome Centers, an adjunct to the library's Adult Learning Center, which has been involved in literacy instruction to adults since 1977. As a one-stop educational facility with social supports, the Welcome Center offers instruction and resource referrals to families whose socioeconomic circumstances often interfere with their learning. Whatever the barrier, the Welcome Center case manager refers students to social services and other community agencies through a network of community partnerships. By leveraging its own free learning resources with the community resources that address the socioeconomic challenges of its students, the Queens Library is removing obstacles to literacy success.

Rana Dajani, the founder of the We Love Reading (WLR) program—which originated in Jordan and has expanded to more than a dozen countries on several continents—developed an innovative model that draws on the volunteer service of women in each of the local communities served. The women, trained by WLR experts, volunteer their time to focus on the read-aloud and storytelling experience to plant the love of reading among children in their neighborhoods and communities.

826 National is a grassroots, community-based program for K–12 students in nine cities. It leverages writing in its afterschool tutoring service to engage students in literacy activities. It also empowers students to publish original work and gain self-confidence. Volunteers, including authors and other celebrities, provide free individual assistance at the storefront centers and publish anthologies of the students' writing to help fund the program (Freeny, 2013).

material, intellectual and emotional features of society or a social group, and that it encompasses, in addition to art and literature, lifestyles, ways of living together, value systems, traditions and beliefs" (p. 1). An individual may belong to several cultures: family, worksite, neighborhood, race, profession, social club, political party, country. Likewise, a group may belong to several cultures; daycare managers may be members of a site staff, a union, a franchise, a state organization, a national organization, and an international organization. Some of these cultures may overlap or even contradict each other, in which case, the individual or group must either live with the disequilibrium or resolve the conflict (i.e., reject one or the other, reject both, or incorporate parts of each).

Culture plays a significant role in community attitudes toward literacy instruction and practice. Hofstede's 1980 model of cultural dimensions provides a useful framework for examining culturally sensitive literacy development.

- *Power distance*. Is the culture highly hierarchical or more egalitarian? Power distance impacts teacher-student relations. For instance, in high power–distance cultures, the teacher is omnipotent and students are not encouraged to ask questions. In low power–distance cultures, teachers and students are considered colearners.
- *Individualism vs. collectivism*. In individualistic cultures, people are likely to belong to several loose-knit groups. Collectivist cultures are well-defined, loyal groups. In collectivist cultures, learners try not to stand out; they might collaborate more willingly than people in individualist cultures.
- *Masculinity*. In some cultures, males are dominant, and societal/career roles are often gendered in terms of achievement, control, power, and remuneration. Depending on how literacy is perceived by the culture, the gender of the literacy expert or teacher might hold a different status. Likewise, in some cultures, education is single-sex. In several cultures, females have less access to literacy education, partly because they have less social status and partly because their job options are limited (Benson, 2005). The United Nations *2030 Agenda for Sustainable Development* include gender equality and quality education for all, which include literacy efforts.
- *Uncertainty avoidance*. Some cultures do not like uncertainty or ambiguity. Some cultures would prefer a ready-made, highly structured, rules-based literacy curriculum, while other cultures would be open to group-developed approaches to literacy development.
- *Long-term vs. short-term orientation*. A long-term orientation is future-oriented, and a short-term orientation is focused on the present or past. Short-term orientation would favor traditional literacy instruction, and long-term orientation would favor open-ended literacy development, such as "learning to learn."

For instance, if a cultural norm about the role of an instructor is to tell students what is right and true, then independent critical evaluation of the information might be discouraged. If a culture values independent thinking and competitiveness, then collaborative efforts might be considered cheating. If the culture believes in a highly structured educational experience, then students may feel lost in loosely defined or student-defined projects. Therefore, literacy projects need to be aware and sensitive to cultural values throughout the planning and implementation stages. In some cases, where obvious discrimination exists, literacy leaders may need to carefully negotiate and incentivize positive change within literacy efforts without threatening the status quo. Hopefully, literacy projects can respect cultural traditions, such as dress and food, or religious observances that do not impinge on learning.

SEALASKA HERITAGE INSTITUTE

Sealaska Heritage Institute is a private nonprofit organization that helps the Tlingit, Haida, and Tsimshian cultures of Southeast Alaska integrate their values into institutions that support them. Their motto is: "We honor our ancestors and pave the way for the future by making heritage a living thing." The institute is guided by a Council of Traditional Schools, a Native Arts Committee, and a Southeast Regional Language Committee. The institute uses several strategies as it promotes cultural diversity and cross-cultural understanding: conducting research, maintaining an archive of Southeast Alaska Native ethnographic material, exhibiting cultural artifacts, producing Alaska's second-largest Native gathering, publishing traditional language resources, and partnering with local schools to promote academic and cultural education (Library of Congress, 2017, p. 11).

LINGUISTIC FACTORS

Closely related to culture is language—particularly in terms of a home language or mother tongue. When the first written language encountered is not the same as the first spoken language, beginning readers are likely to be confused and frustrated. Therefore, literacy instruction should start in the learner's first language. Once the basic reading skills of phonics, syntax, and decoding are understood—how written language "works"—then learning a second language is not as difficult.

Nevertheless, first-language instruction can encounter several challenges. Some countries have one official language: the only one taught formally. This practice undervalues home language and sends a message that such speakers are second class. People who immigrate to another country may speak a language that is uncommon in the target country, and may have difficulty finding home language materials or other people who speak their home language. Additionally, in some areas of the world, very few materials are published because of production and distribution costs. Especially for nonalphabetic writing systems that are used by a small population (such as Naxi in China), mass-producing reading material is problematic. Some languages can be transmitted digitally, which can bypass some production costs; in any case, they require electronic devices that may need internet connectivity. Thus, one solution poses another obstacle.

PRATHAM BOOKS

Pratham Books is one of Indian's largest nonprofit publisher of children's books. In response to the paucity of books in mother tongues and to issues of access and affordability, Pratham's mission has been to "see a book in every child's hand." To that end, since 2004 they have published more than thirty million low-cost books and storycards in twenty Indian languages. To address the increasing use of mobile and other online platforms, Pratham launched StoryWeaver, a repository of multilingual children's stories. StoryWeaver has since crossed 1.5 million users, and offers ten thousand storybooks in one hundred fifty languages on the platform. Supplementing the online text-based stories, Pratham now provides an audiovisual book option called Readalongs, and has also launched Phone Stories. Even with their low-cost materials, some families cannot afford to buy books, so Pratham has a crowdfunding platform, Donate-a-Book, which has resulted in a million books donated to children across India. Furthermore, Pratham has partnered with other groups to lead book events, offer library-in-a-classroom kits, and promote reading champions. (Library of Congress, 2017, p. 6).

Second-language literacy development is challenging for both learners and teachers because often they do not share deep knowledge of each other's fluent language (Wyse, Andrews, & Hoffman, 2010). That issue becomes even more challenging in groups who speak a variety of languages. This situation is further exacerbated because people often acquire basic everyday communication skills, but struggle with academic language. Even the basis for learning a second language (e.g., for work, for social integration, by mandate) and the learning environment can impact literacy development (Ellis, 2009; Krashen, 1981). Therefore, teachers need to consider universal designs for learning by providing multiple means of engagement, of information representation, and of action. Sarkodie-Manash (2000) recommended several other second language-related instructional tips and teaching strategies:

- In all communication, use simple language and short sentences, and avoid idioms. Use meaningful gestures.
- Focus attention on essential vocabulary needed for the specific training or profession. Provide bilingual glossaries and visual references.
- Speak clearly and slowly, without an accent.
- Make documents comprehensible through simpler vocabulary and grammar as well as visual cues. It should be noted that some images may be unrecognizable or demeaning, or may have different meanings to difference cultures.
- Use repetition, paraphrasing, and summaries.
- Use visual aids and graphic organizers to help learners understand content organization and relationships.

- Include frequent comprehension checks and clarification questions.
- If you can't understand a student, don't pretend to.
- Find common topics of interest that are not controversial (for example, the topic of rocks is generally a safe one; birth control would be more controversial).
- Provide opportunities for individual and group work. Pair students linguistically.

The Routledge International Handbook of English, Language and Literacy Teaching, the Canadian journal *Language & Literacy*, and the National Council of Teachers of English journal *Research in the Teaching of English* address many issues of language and literacy in varied educational contexts across the life span and across cultures.

LITERACY VOLUNTEERS OF GREATER HARTFORD (LVGH)

Literacy Volunteers of Greater Hartford (LVGH) is dedicated to adult literacy, providing training in basic literacy, English as a second language, GED (general educational development), and job readiness. Their research-based curricula align with adult education standards, and they partner with other literacy providers and stakeholders to keep current on adult education practices. More recently, the LVGH partnered with the local Brazilian Consulate to teach Brazilian immigrants: English for adults and Brazilian Portuguese for their children. This intergenerational education helps maintain the home culture and facilitates interaction in their new country (Davis, 2014).

EDUCATIONAL FACTORS

Literacy development occurs throughout the community: in formal educational settings such as schools; in informal education such as homes, libraries, social groups; and through the media. Education involves several factors in itself: governance, curricula, resources, personnel, space, time, and assessment.

In some countries, education is controlled at the national level in terms of curricula, finances, and standards for schools and personnel. However, in most countries, education is implemented at the community level—providing the facilities, hiring and monitoring personnel, and assembling the learners. As a subset of education, literacy projects can also be governed at various levels, but they are also more likely to be carried out at the local level. Even international literacy organizations, such as ProLiteracy with its set curriculum, collaborate with nonliteracy and literacy entities to train personnel to teach their communities.

Unlike comprehensive curricula, literacy curricula may be integrated within academic domains or constructed as a stand-alone product and process. While the principles of reading development are generic, the instructional design can vary significantly, largely because of learner needs, literacy educator expertise, and available resources. Literacy projects might use or adapt an existing curriculum, which might be provided by governments, literacy organizations, or commercial enterprises. Sometimes a standardized curriculum is not culturally sensitive, particularly in terms of accompanying resources or specific learners' needs and interests. On the other hand, a standardized curriculum tends to be well tested and validated. Furthermore, designing a curriculum from scratch can be very time-consuming; a better practice is to adapt a literacy curriculum used in the community to align efforts, and to customize as needed to meet learner needs such as second language learners or for workplace literacy. Such customization requires cocreation by partners and target audiences.

As with curricula, resources may blend standardized texts and local material. Often a class will use the same material to optimize group understanding and sharing. Where reading materials are rare, teachers might use single oversize books or posters. Several factors should be considered when selecting literacy materials: alignment to a literacy curriculum, reading level with a range to accommodate the group's spectrum of expertise, age-appropriateness, relevance, ease of use, availability, and cost. As more digital materials are available, equipment to access them is required; the literacy project might need to keep such hardware in one location because of cost or maintenance, although lending portable devices expands the opportunities for learners to practice literacy skills. Other resources include product-centric software such as office suites and audiovisual editing applications. Assistive technologies should also be provided as needed. Creating resources, as with curricula, is labor-intensive. Providing opportunities to create literacy materials to be contributed to the project is an excellent way, if monitored, for learners to demonstrate literacy competency and to deepen their engagement in community literacy efforts.

Teachers constitute the heart of literacy efforts. A range of language, literacy, instructional, and communication skills are needed to teach effective literacy skills, but all teachers and facilitators do need training at some point, and of course often before a literacy project begins.

Instructional designers who shape curricula, instruction, resources, learning activities, and assessment include:

- General teachers who practice developmentally appropriate instructional strategies and can integrate literacy skills with meaningful subject content
- Literacy and reading specialists who can diagnose literacy skills and provide support, including targeted interventions to

struggling learners; specialists can also train teacher generalists specific literacy development techniques

- Tutors and coaches who are trained in specific literacy instructional tasks matched with appropriate learners
- Readers who are trained to share literacy experiences with learners, such as read-alouds and reciprocal teaching
- Writers and media producers who are trained to work with learners to gain writing and production skills that complement reading skills
- Storytellers, singers, and dramatists who are trained to engage learners in oral language development, which can contribute to literacy development
- Parents and other family members who are trained to incorporate literacy activities such as reading directions together, doing singing and wordplay games together, and so on

Even the most willing and literate experts need to be able to interact well with people if they plan to work directly with learners. Otherwise, their expertise might be better used behind the scenes to conduct research, plan logistics, manage technology, or other needed functions. Indeed, many people are needed to support instruction: resource managers, maintenance workers, technology support, business staff, clerical staff, food managers, record-keepers, communications coordinators, transportation personnel, and so on. Coordinating all these personnel requires interpersonal acumen and leadership skills as well.

A curriculum and its delivery exist within some kind of space, be it physical or virtual. Devices with internet connectivity—and stable electric power—are needed for visual learning, which in turn requires a dependable telecommunications infrastructure. Physical space needs at least adequate light and heat, comfortable seating, satisfactory acoustics, some sense of enclosure or separation from outside distractions, and safety; such minimal conditions imply that even a small lea amid trees could serve as a spot for literacy instruction. Classrooms are set up as instructional spaces; they have appropriate seating, working surfaces, writing surfaces, and stable utilities. Other meeting places that might offer space to serve as a learning environment include recreation centers, libraries, religious buildings, agency facilities, factories, corporate meeting rooms, large tents, and even modified transportation containers. A key factor is matching the learning environment to the target audience.

Timing also needs to match the learners' needs and availability. Instruction usually occurs at least monthly in order to maintain momentum and engagement. The length of each session often depends on the attention span of the audience. The length of the total literacy training usually depends on the learning objective. For instance, a targeted intervention might need intensive training for a month or less; early childhood literacy programs might last two years to capture children's significant development; a conversation cafe where people can practice oral literacy skills might be a long-term project; book clubs can exist for decades. Likewise, the day and time of the week needs to accommodate the learners, the teachers, and the space providers, so a preliminary needs assessment will determine a good fit.

Assessment needs to occur throughout the educational process: from an initial needs assessment to a follow-up program evaluation. Assessments need to be built into the educational process in terms of logistics, diagnostics, placement, formative assessment during each learning session, at designative benchmarks, and at culminating points. All the people involved in the educational endeavor need to be assessed in terms of processes and results so that timely modifications can be made for continuous improvement. Furthermore, stakeholders need to know how to access and operate technology for their literacy purposes. Therefore, they may need training to become technologically literate.

COMMONLIT

CommonLit is a nonprofit organization that seeks to ensure that students in grades 3–12—especially those in low-income areas—gain the literacy and problem-solving skills to succeed after graduation. To carry out that charge, CommonLit provides free online access to two thousand reading passages and learning activities in English and Spanish, supported by assessment and monitoring tools as well as teacher professional development. More than seventy thousand schools in the U.S. use CommonLit (Library of Congress, 2017).

TECHNOLOGICAL FACTORS

Technology is playing an increasingly larger role in literacy projects because it expands opportunities to access more literacy materials, offers more flexible ways to deliver literacy experiences, and provides more ways to share literacy. Technology can also attract and engage otherwise nonmotivated learners because of its novelty and access to the world. On the other hand, to take advantage of technology requires education policies, stable telecommunications infrastructure, human and fiscal resources, dependable technical expertise and support, and physical access to devices that can access digital resources (Hanemann & Scarpino, 2016).

If technology is incorporated into literacy projects, the stakeholders need to see its value as early as the beginning planning stages. Because of the specific preconditions for successful technology integration, those elements must be put into the planning timetable. Planners should also consider the need for assistive technology to accommodate learners with special needs such as vision impairment and motor limitations.

PICSTERBOOKS

Picsterbooks leverages technology to help students with hearing limitations learn to read. Specifically, their iDeaf developed interactive book apps provide free storybooks in an interface that includes simplified text and syntax in English and Afrikaans, audio versions of the text, picture animations, and embedded videos showing South African Sign Language interpretations of the text and fingerspelling. Picsterbooks uses engaging stories and focuses more on reading comprehension than phonics. To increase access, Picsterbooks partners with donors to give tablets to schools for the deaf (Davis, 2015).

RUMIE INITIATIVE

The Rumie Initiative is a nonprofit technology organization that removes barriers to literacy in underserved areas by partnering with other organizations to provide children with mobile tablets that are preloaded with lessons and books. Interested groups stipulate the kind of free content to be installed on portable devices, and Rumie locates and stores relevant content on their online repository; the local program administrators can also add to the collection. The customized loaded tablets are sold at cost to the partner organizations around the world: thirty countries by 2020. Students can access materials offline, and teachers can further customize content and monitor student progress on their teacher's tablet (Library of Congress, 2016).

ECONOMIC FACTORS

Funding impacts initial literacy project visioning as well as its plans and implementation. The literacy project's goals and strategies are tied to finances, so the community stakeholders' available funding sources need to be identified to determine the project's viability. The fiscal inventory might result in changing the scope of the project to work within the available budget, but it could also result in requesting more funding in order to accomplish the needed goal.

Economic factors also impact who participates as a learner in literacy projects. For instance, if a fee is required or if learners have to acquire literacy materials or supporting equipment, then on their own their participation may be unfeasible. Sometimes grants or fee waivers can subsidize learners, but asking for such support may be difficult or embarrassing for those needy individuals, so literacy project planners need to think carefully about such options.

For all parties, the ultimate criteria is return on investment. To what degree is the literacy project worth spending money on? For that reason, planners should justify their costs in order to make their case for financial support. They should also consider alternative ways to implement their literacy goals, such as finding free open educational resources, teaming with another project, pilot-testing one phase of the project, or delaying efforts until better economic times.

PHILADELPHIA'S OFFICE OF ADULT EDUCATION (OAE)

The City of Philadelphia's Office of Adult Education (OAE) collaborates with more than eighty adult education and workforce development entities to ensure that all adults can access quality basic education. To that end, the office maintains a database of adult education providers and facilitates enrollment in basic education, GED, and ESL classes convenient to the learner. The office also trains adult educators and provides them technical support. Likewise, the office recruits, trains, and places volunteers to serve as literacy tutors and mentors. In terms of resources, the office oversees free public computing labs and leverages partnerships to maximize appropriate resources. The office's expertise also enables them to influence public policies on adult education (Lamolinara, 2018).

POLITICAL AND GOVERNMENTAL FACTORS

As noted in chapter 3, governments and their agencies can play an important role as partners in literacy projects. Not only might they allocate literacy experts and relevant resources for literacy projects, but they make policies and legislation than can serve as mandates for literacy efforts. As e-government becomes more prevalent, providing services online, the need for literacy becomes more important so government and literacy agendas can align well.

On the other hand, some governments might feel threatened by a literate citizenship who do not agree with government policies and have gained knowledge about alternative ways to govern. In autocratic or dogmatic governments, functional literacy may be acceptable but advanced literacy and the production of independent ideas might be stifled. A government might also downplay literacy for females and certain groups such as immigrants or individuals with special needs. Literacy programs might also be considered examples of neocolonialism—when sponsored by UNESCO or the World Bank, for instance—and treated with distain or distrust (Wickens & Sandlin, 2007). In such cases, early childhood literacy projects, second-language programs, and basic literacy projects would probably get more governmental support.

Politics are associated with groups of people with common agendas and ideologies. Unlike governments that are organizational bodies that have power by law, political structures have a much broader base and try to influence decision-makers. Politics can be found in almost any group, as a way to influence others; it is more process-based. Politics can enter into literacy projects from the start, as groups try to drive the literacy agenda to satisfy their own agenda. Politicians, especially those who want to gain power and recognition, may use literacy as a campaign issue. Literacy project planners can leverage such endorsements, but they need to carefully examine the politician's reputation, influence, commitment, and possible hidden agenda or "strings" before giving that person a venue for publicity. In the final analysis, the community's literacy needs should be the basis for planning, and any governmental or political group would have to agree to the project's stipulations. The literacy project should be in control, not the politics.

NEW YORK CITY DEPARTMENT OF HOMELESS SERVICES (DHS)

The New York City Department of Homeless Services (DHS) partnered with area public libraries to address the literacy needs of children experiencing homelessness. The pilot project established library services in thirty shelters. Each site included a collection of reading materials in a safe, secure area. Library workers visited the shelters to promote literacy through library card drives, storyhours, tutoring, and book discussion groups. In addition, literacy instruction workshops empowered parents to get involved in their children's education (Library of Congress, 2016).

REFERENCES

Benson, C. (2005). *Girls, educational equity and mother tongue–based teaching.* Bangkok, Thailand: UNESCO Bangkok. Asia and Pacific Regional Bureau for Education.

Davis, J. (2015). *Library of Congress literacy awards 2015: Best practices.* Washington, DC: Library of Congress.

Davis, J. (2014). *Library of Congress literacy awards 2014: Best practices.* Washington, DC: Library of Congress.

Ellis, R. (2009). *The study of second language acquisition.* Oxford, UK: Oxford University Press.

Freeny, M. (2013). *Library of Congress literacy awards 2013: Best practices.* Washington, DC: Library of Congress.

Gambrell, L. B. (1996). Creating classroom cultures that foster reading motivation. *Reading Teacher, 50,* 14–25.

Habibian, M. et al. (2015). The impact of training metacognitive strategies on reading comprehension among ESL learners. *Journal of Education and Practice, 6*(28), 61–69.

Hanemann, U., & Scarpino, C. (2016). *Harnessing the potential of ICTs.* Paris, France: UNESCO.

Hofstede, G. (1980). *Culture consequences.* London, UK: Sage.

Krashen, S. (1981). *Second language acquisition and second language learning.* New York: Pergamon Press.

Lamolinara, G. (2018). *Library of Congress literacy awards 2018.* Washington, DC: Library of Congress.

Library of Congress. (2017). *Library of Congress literacy awards 2017.* Washington, DC: Library of Congress.

Library of Congress. (2016). *Library of Congress literacy awards 2016.* Washington, DC: Library of Congress.

Nashville Public Library. (2013). *Blueprint for early childhood success.* Nashville, TN: Nashville Public Library. https://static1.squarespace.com/static/57752cbed1758e541bdeef6b/t/5aa96f38e4966b90348be dd4/1521053514961/Full-Report.pdf.

Sarkodie-Manash, K. (Ed.). (2000). *Reference services for the adult learner.* New York, NY: Haworth Press.

Schutte, N. S., & Malouff, J. M. (2007). Dimensions of reading motivation: Development of an adult reading motivation scale. *Reading Psychology, 28*(5), 469–489.

UNESCO. (2002). *Universal declaration on cultural diversity.* The Hague, Netherlands: UNESCO.

Wickens, C. M., & Sandlin, J. A. (2007). Literacy for what? Literacy for whom? The politics of literacy education and neocolonialism in UNESCO- and World Bank–sponsored literacy programs. *Adult Education Quarterly, 57*(4), 275–292.

Wyse, D., Andrews, R., & Hoffman, J. (Eds.). (2010). *The Routledge international handbook of English, language and literacy teaching.* New York, NY: Routledge.

5

Applied Literacies

Literacy doesn't exist in a vacuum, so literacy projects often contextualize literacy in terms of other lifelong activities, such as health and money management. Such linkages incentivize individuals to participate in educational experiences that can improve their lives. The premise is that a concrete reason to read—and meaningful positive reading success—can lead to lifelong reading habits. Another way to frame these concrete literacies is to posit that they all fall under the umbrella of information literacy: the ability to locate, access, evaluate, use, manage, and communicate information effectively and responsibly. This chapter considers five applied literacies that provide relevant contexts for learners: health, fiscal, ecological, media, and cultural.

HEALTH LITERACY

As the World Health Organization (WHO) asserted, "literacy and health literacy are fundamental components of pursuing health and well-being in modern society. As societies grow more complex and people are increasingly bombarded with health information and misinformation and confront complex health care systems, becoming a health-literate person has become a growing challenge" (Kickbusch et al., 2013, p. iv). Health literacy may be as simple as reading food and medical labels and as complicated as determining health insurance options. Not only does health literacy affect someone's personal health and the health of their family, but it also influences their workplace and community. Governments are deeply invested in health literacy, as it impacts preventative and curative medical resources and support; health literacy can also help bridge equity gaps of minority and migrant populations. A healthy population is a productive population. In fact, health literacy is so important for the community that WHO founded a European healthy cities movement to promote health literacy; healthy cities continuously improve physical and social environments, expand their resources, and enact supportive policies to improve community health literacy so people can make healthy choices.

The World Health Organization defined health literacy as entailing "people's knowledge, motivation and competencies to access, understand, appraise and apply health information to make judgements and take decisions in everyday life concerning health care, disease prevention and health promotions to maintain or improve quality of life" (Kickbusch et al., 2013, p. 4). Several stakeholders are involved in health literacy: the general public, community-based organizations, health professionals, government agencies, educators, businesses, faith-based organizations, and media outlets. The *European Health Literacy Survey* identified three levels of health services: health care, disease prevention, and health promotion. Literacy involves health behavior in light of health services. Those services need to consider costs in providing sustainable efforts that equitably empower their users (Sorensen et al., 2012).

While everyone needs information about health, the level of health literacy varies significantly between different populations. For instance, people with less education and less income tend to be less health-literate. Older people and migrants are also less likely to be health-literate. Furthermore, health literacy can vary due to context and culture, according to the World Health Organization. In the United States, only 12 percent of adults have proficient health literacy, and 14 percent have below-basic health literacy. To make matters worse, health information is often written at a higher reading level than most general texts, such as magazines (U.S. Department of Health and Human Services, Office of Disease Prevention and Health Promotion, 2010).

Health education tries to anticipate the information needs of its target audience, combined with educators' perceived desired health outcomes, encompassing both preventative measures and interventions. Health literacy education can be delivered in formal educational settings or informal venues such as workplaces, libraries, or wherever people congregate. Policies usually dictate formal educational curricula and supporting resources, including qualified instructors. Advocacy groups such as health providers and parents can serve as catalysts for addressing health literacy. Informal education can sometimes be more effective, as it is likely to link training concretely with real-life situations. For instance, parenting classes are good venues to talk about growing a family culture of reading; stores can provide guidance on how to read nutritional labels;

sports training often includes exercises to keep athletes healthy; and social services to new immigrants can address health agency support. Adults sometimes prefer to receive health information informally—particularly through community education, because it may be more culturally sensitive or more in line with social norms (Fennell & Escue, 2013). In any case, using these settings offers opportunities to share health information and teach people how to access, comprehend, and apply that information effectively. If for no other reason, health education is needed to help individuals learn about credible health websites and how to evaluate health information.

Health literacy education can target three populations: health consumers, health providers, and health intermediaries (i.e., health-literate laypeople who help health consumers). The base competencies include information literacy to find relevant information; digital literacy to navigate the internet; numeracy to measure medications and understand health plans; communication skills to share personal information; health conceptual knowledge, such as anatomy, well-being, factors impacting health (e.g., diseases and injuries), and self-care, as well as understanding the health care system (U.S. Department of Health and Human Services, 2010). However, gaining health literacy faces several obstacles, including physical access to information, language issues, reading literacy issues, cultural attitudes, distrust of information or information provider.

Health professionals already have concept knowledge. Their focus needs to be in communication skills and cultural attitudes toward health. For instance, the Agency for Healthcare Research and Quality within the U.S. Department of Health and Human Services offered an online training course for health providers: Unified Health Communication 101: Addressing Health Literacy, Cultural Competency, and Limited English Proficiency (http://www.hrsa.gov/publichealth/healthliteracy/). The goal was to improve patient communication skills to help patients gain health literacy. Part of instruction included improving the usability of health information in the following ways: by getting to know and respect clients, conducting pre- and post-tests, checking for understanding, communicating in plain language and short messages, complementing language with images, using universal signage, and using translators (U.S. Department of Health and Human Services, 2010).

Health intermediaries act as a go-between for purveyors of health information and a person seeking health help; such intermediaries might include counselors, youth-serving agencies, library workers, families, and friends. Their occupation generally is not in the field of health, but they may have personal health experience or interest, and usually serve as trusted frontline information sharers (Abrahamson et al., 2008). These linkers need to know about the health profession and that particular community's needs for health literacy, as well as current community information-seeking practices and health resources.

Such knowledge is often reflected in librarians' work. In their role as intermediaries, librarians would do well to follow the recommendations derived from the literature (Burke & Hughes-Hassell, 2007; Crutzen, 2010; Lariscy, Reber & Paek, 2011):

- Identify information seekers' health interests and start interaction with them by providing resources that engage their attention.
- Locate and provide social media sources about health information; for example, the Centers for Disease Control uses podcasts, widgets, e-cards, content syndication, and digital badges (http://www.cdc.gov/socialmedia/).
- Maintain a list of community health agencies that are user-friendly.
- Provide health-related programming in schools, libraries, and community centers—for example, a program on body image in the media, featuring testimonials on eating disorders, workshops on ways to relieve stress, and athletes talking about healthy exercise.
- Identify people who can help clientele find health information.
- Tailor communication to specific demographics. For example, with teen groups, use text messaging, promote word of mouth, use videos.
- Personalize information by knowing how each person likes to get and process information. Identify reading levels and the amount of information needed.
- Incorporate self-tests, asking questions such as "How healthy do you eat?" and "How do you know when it's safe to have sex?"
- Link health issues, such as drug use and unprotected sex. Align your communication with cultural and gender expectations; for instance, have males-only sessions or provide written materials rather than group discussion for Muslim females.

Librarians reflect a wide spectrum of health expertise as well as attitudes about their role as health intermediaries. Even in those cases where librarians do not feel comfortable as intermediaries because of their lack of health knowledge (Kelly, 2012), they can share information and their digital literacy expertise to train and partner with other intermediaries who have close proximity to the person needing information as well as more health expertise. Librarians can also provide outreach services to information intermediaries as a way to indirectly serve the ultimate target audience. A person who is not health-literate might need to be information literate enough to know whether to trust the knowledge of a health intermediary or health professional.

REACH OUT AND READ

Reach Out and Read is a national network of clinicians who support early childhood literacy through well-child checkups. Starting at six months and continuing each six months until children are 3 years old, health professionals give the family a developmentally appropriate book and teach parents how to engage their children in literacy activities. To supplement these visits, Reach Out and Read provides virtual reading and live events, and offers two hundred free resources to download. To gain that expertise, health professionals are trained on a research-based early childhood literacy model. More than six thousand health sites, located in every U.S. state, participate in Reach Out and Read's program, and almost five million children are served each year (Freeny, 2013).

The U.S. Office of Disease Prevention and Health Promotion (2019) recognized that health literacy and health behaviors are influenced by internal and external factors, and community-based programs can reach people outside of traditional healthcare systems. Such local social structures can provide more customized, authentic information and education that can change community norms and institute new community policies and practices. To that end, the Agency for Health Research and Quality developed a toolkit for health literacy education (Brega et al., 2015). They provided the following tips for improving community health literacy through education.

1. Form a team of stakeholders and health literacy experts.
2. Create a health literacy improvement plan by assessing current health literacy levels and available resources to increase health literacy.
3. Raise community awareness about health-literacy needs and benefits.
4. Assess, select, and create easy-to-understand materials.
5. Address language differences.
6. Consider culture, customs, and beliefs.
7. Provide instruction using clear communication, welcoming interaction, feedback, and follow-up action.
8. Help people make action plans.
9. Help patients remember how and when to take their medications.
10. Improve supportive systems through referrals, connections to non-medical support, and links to medical resources.

Recognizing the vital role that women play in health behaviors, in 2016 UNESCO's Institute for Lifelong Learning produced a publication focused on health and literacy for women's empowerment. The institute stated that adult literacy programs that incorporate health should use a holistic approach that addresses socioeconomic and cultural equity and other needed changes.

The agency recommended several health-related themes: maternal and child health, community health and nutrition, HIV/AIDS prevention, and mental health and well-being. The institute also compiled a set of good educational practices: identifying and understanding appropriate target groups, building on learners' experiences and local knowledge, promoting critical literacy approaches, responding to specific contexts, leveraging technology, promoting empowerment at any point, and building sustainability.

The following resources provide valuable information about health literacy education.

Centers for Disease Control and Prevention. *Health literacy resources.* https://www.cdc.gov/healthliteracy/learn/Resources.html.

Farmer, L. (2019). *ICT literacy in health sciences.* Long Beach, CA: MERLOT. https://contentbuilder.merlot.org/toolkit/html/snapshot.php?id=9514883793438677.

Health Resources & Services Administration. (2019). *Health literacy.* Washington, DC: U.S. Department of Health and Human Services. https://www.hrsa.gov/about/organization/bureaus/ohe/health-literacy/index.html.

McCale, N. (2019). *Health literacy and patient education guide: Health literacy.* Denver, CO: University of Colorado. https://hslibraryguides.ucdenver.edu/healthliteracy.

Save the Children. *Global health technical and policy resources.* https://www.savethechildren.org/us/about-us/resource-library/health-library.

UNESCO. *SDG resources for educators—good health and well-being.* https://en.unesco.org/themes/education/sdgs/material/03.

U.S. National Library of Medicine. *MEDLINE/PubMed search and health literacy information resources.* https://www.nlm.nih.gov/services/queries/health_literacy.html.

FISCAL LITERACY

Managing money is a key skill that changes in practice throughout one's life: from handling an allowance to starting a business to planning for retirement. Yet many people have difficulty spending, budgeting, and investing, particularly in a consumer society that entices people to spend more than they have and as financial choices have become more complex. Especially in times of economic downturn or during a personal crisis such as unemployment or having health problems, dealing with money—or the lack of it—can lead to despairing consequences, including homelessness. For society as a whole, financial security is a cornerstone for a stable government. It is no wonder that financial literacy is becoming a priority for decision-makers and educators.

What, then, constitutes financial literacy? The World Bank stated: "People who are financially literate have the ability to make informed financial choices regarding saving, investing, borrowing, and more" (Klapper, Lusardi, & van

Oudheusden, 2015, p. 4). The World Bank also identified four fundamental concepts in fiscal decision-making: knowledge of basic numeracy, of interest rates and compounding, of inflation, and of risk diversification. Using those concepts to measure financial literacy, the World Bank surveyed more than 150,000 people in 140 economies and found that country-level financial literacy ranged from 71 percent down to 13 percent. Overall, only a third of adults understood basic financial concepts. Having a bank account and using credit deepened financial skills. Women, the poor, and the less education suffered the most from lack of financial literacy.

In 2003, the Organisation for Economic Co-operation and Development (OECD) created a financial education initiative, and in 2008 established the International Network on Financial Education. By 2015 sixty countries had developed national strategies for financial literacy education. These programs try to improve consumer awareness of economic and financial realities to make responsible fiscal decisions. To create these strategies, the OECD recommended the following steps.

1. Diagnose the population's needs and fiscal behaviors, existing financial education initiatives, and circumstances, including resources.
2. Establish institutional and governing arrangements such as mandates, politics, and structures.
3. Set evidence-based goals, core competence objectives, and action plans.
4. Fund and implement action plans through multichannel delivery, harnessing existing learning environments, and supporting individual and community engagement and decision-making.
5. Monitor and evaluate action plans.

Such education may aim to be apolitical and neutral, but politics and other people in power do impact economic decisions, so understanding such influencers and gaining collective agency is an important aspect of financial literacy.

In 2013 the Council for Economic Education developed a set of national standards for teaching personal finance in K–12 education. Their concepts included earning income, buying goods and services, using credit, saving, financial investing, and protecting and insuring finances. But these standards are seldom integrated into formal educational curricula. Increasingly, the United States is incorporating fiscal literacy into K–12 curricula. However, a review of financial education programs found negligible impact on learner fiscal behavior (Fernandes, Lynch, & Netemeyer, 2014). The researchers made several recommendations to improve fiscal literacy education:

- Address soft skills such as strategic planning and taking investment risks.
- Provide just-in-time education for specific decisions.
- Provide immediate, specific feedback and employ targeted interventions to correct fiscal behaviors.

- For emotionally controlled decisions, point out the problematic behavior and teach self-control.
- Narrow the learner scope so fiscal literacy can closely align with the learners' needs at a particular stage of life (e.g., becoming new parents, nearing retirement) or a specific, predictable financial decision (e.g., buying a first home, choosing a 401[k] plan).
- For youth, provide immediate opportunities to apply fiscal literacy.

The U.S. Financial Literacy and Education Commission (2019) identified best practices for generic financial literacy education, with specific recommendations for higher education. General practices include: knowing the individuals and families to be served; building on motivation; providing actionable, relevant, and timely information; improving the public's key financial skills of locating, interpreting, and acting on financial information; facilitating good decisions and follow-through; providing ongoing support; evaluating for impact; and developing standards for professional educators. College students need additional information on student borrowing and repayment of loans, the importance of graduation, and financial obligations upon graduating. The commission also recommended using peer educators and addressing financial topics frequently in both formal and informal educational settings.

In reviewing the research about financial education, Willis (2013) found that financial education does not lead to household financial well-being at a significant level. She cited several barriers to effective financial education: the changing dynamics of the financial marketplace, information and choice overload, lack of numeracy and linguistic literacy, lack of self-control and rational behavior, short-term thinking, overconfidence from having partial fiscal literacy, lack of just-in-time training (as in the middle of an escrow negotiation), and insufficient income and assets to leverage fiscal literacy. Willis suggested some ways to complement fiscal literacy education: math instruction, financial counseling, criteria for evaluating financial advisors, and just-in-time help with financial forms, such as college financial aid.

Fiscal literacy offers a golden opportunity for community partnerships between educators and financial institutions such as banks, realtors, insurers, and financial planners. These partnerships can facilitate embedding financial education into the workplace and other community spaces. Collaborating with financial institutions not only gives the training credibility, but it also facilitates learner access and practice with real financial resources. Furthermore, collaboration helps financial institutions gain more stability with informed customers.

For instance, libraries provide community spaces and information expertise to foster fiscal literacy through providing objective, authoritative, current sources and ensuring privacy in communicating with patrons about financial information. Libraries are also natural partners—they understand the importance of mutual benefit; of partnerships with organizations rather

RURAL EDUCATION AND DEVELOPMENT NEPAL (READ NEPAL)

Rural Education and Development Nepal (READ Nepal) builds literacy and economic development through establishing community libraries. One or more businesses are then responsible for maintaining support for each library. The libraries include sections for different types of users, and provide a Practical Answers program that collects and answers a wide variety of topics such as law, health, and agriculture. In partnership with local organizations, the libraries also serve as community centers for literacy education and development training such as job skills and economic empowerment (Davis, 2014).

than individuals; of preventing solicitations; of providing learning options, formal agreements, and ongoing communication; of sharing target audiences; of sharing contributions to activities; of building on success; and of measuring outcomes (Reference and User Services Association, 2014).

When the British National Research and Development Centre (Coben, Dawes, & Lee, 2005) surveyed these collaborative fiscal trainings, they discovered that most programs were delivered as a context for literacy or as a response to a perceived need (e.g., debt problems, financial exclusion). The education was more impactful in the context of deprivation, vulnerability, and poverty than in a high-income context. The researchers also noticed that employers were wary about providing authorized financial advice or being perceived as intrusive in employees' lives, so partnering with outside institutions was more acceptable for all parties. Some of the potential partners identified in the study included governmental agencies, housing associations, private sector businesses, credit unions, trade unions, nonprofit organizations, and consumer protection organizations. The researchers also recognized that individuals might not take advantage of financial education for several reasons: prior negative educational experience, lack of awareness of need or available offerings, lack of relevant topics, distrust of the information provider, inconvenient location or timing, limited literacy or language, and a preference for more "passive" information delivery methods such as the internet, media outlets, and publications. Financial education providers need to address their target audience's needs and perceptions when negotiating partnership logistics such as funding, setting, staffing, content, delivery method, and accreditation.

The following resources provide valuable information about fiscal literacy education.

Australian Government. *National financial literacy strategy.* https://financialcapability .gov.au/.

Consumer Financial Protection Bureau. https://www.consumerfinance.gov/.

Federal Deposit Insurance Corporation. *Financial education.* https://www.fdic.gov/ consumers/education/.

Government of Canada. Financial Consumer Agency of Canada. https://www.canada
.ca/en/financial-consumer-agency.html.

Iconomix. *Economics in the classroom*. https://www.iconomix.ch/en/.

LINCS. *Resources by topic: Financial literacy*. https://lincs.ed.gov/professional
-development/resource-collections/by-topic/Financial%20Literacy.

Mint. *Ultimate resources for teaching kids about money*. https://www.mint.com/
ultimate-resources-for-teaching-kids-about-money.

Moneyforce. *Tools to help you get money fit*. https://www.moneyforce.org.uk/.

Moneysense. *Financial health check*. https://www.moneysense.gov.sg/.

National Credit Union Administration. *Financial literacy & education resource center*.
https://www.ncua.gov/consumers/financial-literacy-resources.

National Education Association. *Resources for teaching financial literacy*. http://www
.nea.org/tools/lessons/resources-for-teaching-financial-literacy.html.

National Endowment for Financial Education. *Education*. https://www.nefe.org/
education/default.aspx.

OECD. *International gateway for financial education*. http://www.oecd.org/financial/
education/.

Practical Money Skills. *Resources*. https://www.practicalmoneyskills.com/resources.

Public Library Association. *Financial literacy*. http://www.ala.org/pla/resources/tools/
programming-instruction/financial-literacy.

U.S. Financial Literacy and Education Commission. *My Money.gov*. http://www
.mymoney.gov.

ENVIRONMENTAL LITERACY/ECOLITERACY

Humans have always impacted the earth they live on: killing other animals, cutting down trees, causing pollution, extracting oil and minerals. How can humans have a sustainable relationship with the biosphere? That is the underlying issue for environmental literacy, ecological literacy, and ecoliteracy (McBride et al., 2013). Generally, environmental literacy consists of an awareness and concern about the environment and its issues, along with the knowledge, skills, and motivation to solve those problems and prevent new ones. Ecological literacy focuses more on systems thinking based on ecological knowledge. Ecoliteracy intends to create sustainable human communities. Most environmental-literacy educational frameworks include basic knowledge of ecological concepts, environmental sensitivity and appreciation, understanding of ecological-cultural interactions, awareness of environmental issues, and skills and behaviors to prevent or resolve those issues. In any case, it takes knowledge and action to maintain a sustainable environment, and only a third of American have basic environmental knowledge (Reynolds, Brondizio, & Robinson, 2010).

In 2011, the North American Association for Environmental Education developed a framework for assessing environmental literacy. They identified three components of environmental literacy:

1. Competencies: identify, analyze, and investigate environmental issues; evaluate and make judgments about environmental issues; defend positions and resolve issues using evidence and knowledge; create and evaluate plans to resolve environmental issues
2. Knowledge: of physical and ecological systems, sociocultural and political systems, environment issues and solutions, and citizen participation and action
3. Dispositions: sensitivity, worldview, personal responsibility, self-efficacy, motivations, and intentions.

The association also identified five categories of civic action: ecomanagement, persuasion, consumer/economic action, political action, and legal action.

A Delphi research method for conceptualizing environmental literacy (Kaya & Elster, 2019) resulted in the following definition:

> knowing and understanding environmental issues; having attitudes, concerns, morals, and ethics towards the environment; having the ability and intention to act with environmentally responsible behavior; having the active involvement and social engagement related to the environment, as well as having skills to evaluate data and draw conclusions to form one's own opinion and collaboratively working with stakeholders to solve environmental issues. (p. 1580)

They also identified several subdimensions (environmental issues, attitudes, motivation, ethics, environmentally friendly intent and behavior, sustainability) when evaluating environmental literacy. The group identified the follow curricular topics: environmental perceptions, environmentally friendly behavior, environmental concepts, environmental problems and solutions, sustainability, and social perspectives. In terms of instructional approach, the group recommended project-based learning, discussion methods, out-of-school activities, and collaborative learning. They also thought that pre- and in-service teacher training was key for developing environment-literate individuals. Furthermore, the group stated that environmental literacy education should be supported by the community stakeholders—government, organizations, families, and the media.

Reynolds, Brondizio, and Robinson (2010) at Arizona State University posited that environmental literacy encompasses knowledge about the natural environment, human economic and social systems' interaction with the natural environment, and the skills and ethics to apply this understanding to life choices that promote sustainable human communities and ecological systems. Based on this definition, the university developed three themes for teaching environmental literacy: human dependence on ecosystems, human domination of ecosystems (ecological footprint), and human stewardship of ecosystems (sustainability). The university also developed strategies for teaching environmental literacy: solving real-world problems, analyzing global environment impacts of everyday life (through life-cycle analysis of family objects such as bicycles and notebook paper), visiting nature preserves and human-altered landscapes, and using service learning for students to conceptualize their place in the world and their relations to it. The cross-disciplinary aspects of environmental literacy spur collaborative efforts, not only across academic domains but also as community-wide initiatives.

Scholz and Gallati (2011) defined environmental literacy as "the capacity to perceive, appropriately interpret, and value the specific state, dynamics, and potential of the environmental system, as well as to take appropriate action to maintain, restore, or improve these states" (p. xviii). The researchers asserted that managing environmental problems requires analyzing human systems that impact the material environment, understanding the environment and human-environment interaction, and generating solutions for sustainable development. Several disciplines contribute to these understandings, including biology, psychology, sociology, economics, and industrial ecology.

Environmental literacy helps learners gain knowledge about both the environment and themselves in terms of their impact on and their responsibility to their surroundings. Therefore, environmental literacy education should emphasize personal relevance and choice in subject matter and projects (Randall, 2019). The researcher, who focused on higher education, noted that students who took the environmental literacy course were already interested in the topic, so institutions as a whole should consider encouraging such education more strongly, to the point that it be considered as a graduation requirement.

A special issue the *EURASIA Journal of Mathematics, Science and Technology Education* (2019) featured environmental literacy in K–12 science classrooms. Researchers found that Australian teachers had little guidance in sustainability ideas, and needed professional development to help them evaluate and address their students' understanding of complex environmental issues. Those in-service courses included computational thinking, systems thinking, socio-scientific reasoning, and authentic experiential learning. The other side of the coin, instructing students in environmental literacy, included inquiry process, data exploration, gamification, constructing environmental arguments, and incorporating technology.

Varela-Losada et al. (2016) reviewed environmental education in two major associated journals for possible trends, which included cross-curricular education, student-centered active learning, connecting with student needs and interests, social learning, focus on real issues through outdoor and other experiential learning, incorporation of ICT (information and communication technology) literacy, and paying attention to environment-society relationships and processes more than results. The researchers did not see much explicit mention of critical thinking or independent decision-making, although those researchers saw the need to help students gain such skills. In addition, only a third of the studies involved community improvement, and only a handful of efforts involved members of the community. The researchers pointed out the impact of service learning on pro-environmental attitudes and collaborative behaviors.

UNESCO (Hanemann & UNESCO, 2015) noted that many literacy programs incorporate environmental topics and a few have focused on environmental sustainability and the safe-guarding of environmental, social, and economic well-being in the long term. For instance, an Indonesian program helped a community prepare for natural disasters as part of their literacy program. The Cairo Garbage City Programme blends literacy with environmentally conscious entrepreneurship. In Nigeria's Edo state, adult literacy education incorporated environmental literacy content (Norris & Osayande, 2017). As a result of their education, the students had a more positive attitude toward the environment, which correlated weakly with their environmental behavior. The researchers recommended adding environmental education to all literacy education in the state. In Jordanian communities, social stories about environmental issues helped children gain literacy competencies and practice more ecological electrical and water consumption behaviors (Mahasneh, Romanowski, & Dajani, 2017).

The following resources provide valuable information about environmental literacy education.

Environmental Education Research. https://www.tandfonline.com/loi/ceer20.
Environmental Literacy Council. *Teaching resources.* https://enviroliteracy.org/teaching-resources/.
International Journal of Environmental and Science Education. http://www.ijese.net/.
Journal of Environmental Education. https://www.tandfonline.com/toc/vjee20/current.
Ten Strands. *Environmental literacy resources.* https://tenstrands.org/envirolitresources/.
UNESCO. *Sustainable development goals—resources for educators.* https://en.unesco.org/themes/education/sdgs/material/.

MEDIA LITERACY

Mass media play an increasingly significant role in today's society. Even when one is not searching for information, mass media permeate everyone's environment, influencing their worldview and decision-making. Therefore, people need to consciously and critically analyze and evaluate mass media messages and only then decide how to respond. Otherwise, they will not make reasoned decisions, and they will suffer the consequences of their assumptions or ignorance. They must be media literate.

Media literacy has two prongs: (1) the concept of an information format (e.g., print, audio, digital) and its impact on meaning; and (2) mass media (e.g., television, film, radio, periodicals) and their impact. Both address a literacy framework to access, analyze, evaluate, create, and engage with messages in a variety of forms. Media literacy builds an understanding of the role of media in society as well as the essential skills of inquiry and self-expression necessary for citizens of a democracy (Grizzle et al., 2014).

Many people feel comfortable using media for entertainment or communicating with friends, but they often do not have academic, technical, and critical thinking skills or know-how to express themselves effectively online in public discourse. On the other hand, when people use the internet to exchange information, they are more likely to be civically engaged, which can apply to media (Harshman, 2017).

A growing case has been made for media literacy education—to critically evaluate news and other current information, to understand the media production process, to generate media, to interpret cross-cultural media, and to facilitate civic engagement. Especially as people tend to get their news online, they need to know how media messages are produced and how these messages impact society. People also need to know how to respond to media messages and leverage media to voice their own thoughts.

The National Association for Media Literacy Education (2007) identified six core principles for such education:

1. Active inquiry and critical thinking about media
2. A need to address all forms of media
3. Building on and reinforcing other lifelong literacy skills
4. Development of civic engagement
5. Media as part of culture and a socialization agent
6. Individual construction of meaning from media messages.

Silverblatt, Ferry, and Finan (2015) suggested five approaches to teach media literacy: ideological analysis based on cultural studies; autobiographical analysis; nonverbal analysis (paralanguage); mythic analysis (allegories and belief systems); and analysis of production elements, such as visual principles and editing practices.

In synthesizing factors that lead to successful media literacy programs, Hobbs (2010) noted the importance of community-level media literacy initiatives, outreach and stakeholder engagement, teacher education partnerships,

---

POWER POETRY

Power Poetry, which started in 2012, is the first and largest mobile/online teen poetry community. Its function is to leverage reading and writing poetry to promote literacy and empower teens and young adults. Teachers register to start a poetry group on the organization's safe online platform. Power Poetry provides teachers with free resources to guide students in a creative environment and link with other online Power Poetry groups. Students create, "workshop," present, and publish poetry. In addition, mentors are available to critique and foster skills development (Davis, 2014).

---

and research and assessment. She recommended several practices to advance media literacy.

- Map existing community media literacy resources and help underwrite community partnerships to integrate media literacy into existing programs.
- Create a media literacy youth corps in underserved communities via museums, libraries, and community centers.
- Create school system–wide media literacy projects in partnership with communities and media outlets.
- Produce videos of effective media literacy instruction to build teacher expertise.
- Encourage the media industry to create shared social norms through developing and disseminating media products about ethnical behaviors in using media.
- Provide public venues for community-produced media competitions and showcases, especially promoting or advancing media literacy.

Community engagement in media literacy can start on a small scale—even at the level of students observing their community. Hobbs (2013) recounted a situation in which her elementary students accidentally encountered a person experiencing homelessness. The children's questions led to research on homelessness, including analyzing news media and film. The students then interviewed community leaders and advocates for the homeless. Based on the information gathered, the students created a class multimedia project about the community's homeless issue.

In another community setting (Charmaraman, 2013), urban teens collectively wrote and produced prosocial videos based on their neighborhood experiences, which they showed at community screenings. The project particularly benefited urban minority youth who had limited resources and social capital to combat the negative stereotypes foisted upon them. This youth development afterschool program empowered the participants, and it increased their willingness and ability to help improve their own community through a greater sense of voice and collective impact.

At the other end of the education spectrum is an example of service learning. Crandall (2016) teaches a graduate-level media literacy elective that culminates in students designing and implementing a community-action research project for social change. Particularly because the projects begin with student voices and problems that students wanted to solve, the students see themselves as members of the community and as change agents within that community.

The latter approach works particularly well in community-based media arts education: gaining media competency through producing media products. When learners approach media literacy through a professional-production perspective, they gain opportunities for creative self-expression and self-reflection through critical analysis. Furthermore, many community production venues are small enough to tailor their programs to fit the needs of their learner populations and bypass more formal educational parameters (Grauer, Castro, & Lin, 2012). These informal educational settings foster agency for their learners, many of whom might be otherwise disenfranchised. In examining film production–based youth media–intensive programs, Grauer, Castro, and Lin observed how filmmaking taught communication and collaboration, advanced self-identities, and resulted in higher academic achievement.

As one way to address media literacy, UNESCO (Muratova & Grizzle, 2019) focused on the role of journalists. The authors pointed out the need for journalists to focus on the media literacy needs of their audiences, and to create media content that teaches those competencies in collaboration with media literacy experts. Such efforts can enable citizens to partner with journalists to develop and disseminate media messages.

Today's news, in particular, is a wake-up call for communities to gain competency in critically analyzing media specifically and information in general. Stakeholders can leverage this hot topic to highlight the importance of media literacy and incorporate it systematically into formal and informal education so that community members will be better prepared as informed citizens and can participate more effectively in civic action.

The following resources provide valuable information about media literacy education.

Center for Media Literacy. *How to teach media literacy.* https://www.medialit.org/how-teach-media-literacy.

EAVI: Media Literacy and Citizenship. https://eavi.eu.

Evens Foundation. https://issuu.com/evensfoundation.

Index of Media Literacy Research. http://mediataitokoulu.fi/index.php?lang=fi.

IREX Europe. https://irex-europe.fr/.

Journal of Media Literacy Education. https://namle.net/publications/journal-of-media
-literacy-education/.

KQED. *Media literacy*. https://ww2.kqed.org/education/media-literacy/.

Media & Information Literacy Clearinghouse. https://milunesco.unaoc.org/.

Media Education Lab. *Teaching resources*. https://mediaeducationlab.com/curriculum/
materials.

MediaInAction. *Resource bank*. http://mediainaction.eu/resources/.

Media Literacy Clearinghouse. http://frankwbaker.com/mlc/.

Media Literacy Now. *Education resources*. https://medialiteracynow.org/resources/.

National Association for Media Literacy Education. http://namle.net.

CULTURAL LITERACY

Globalization impacts people's lives—and the preparation for those life choices. People are more likely to migrate so that many communities have become more diverse. Therefore, communities as a whole need to become culturally competent: open to learning about other cultures and sharing one's own culture, able to change personal perspectives, and able to communicate effectively across cultures.

When people come together to form stable groups with sustained shared value/belief systems and normative expectations/behaviors, they comprise a culture. UNESCO (2002) defines culture as "the set of distinctive spiritual, material, intellectual and emotional features of society or a social group, and that it encompasses, in addition to art and literature, lifestyles, ways of living together, value systems, traditions and beliefs" (p. 1). Both groups and individuals may belong to several cultures, determined by geographic area, race, profession, social club, and the like. Again, when these cultures overlap or contradict each other, the individual or group must either live with the disequilibrium or resolve the conflict.

This tension between cultures applies especially to migrant populations. Not only does each ethnic group have its own identity, but immigrants who come into a country as refugees have an additional identity to confront and may have to overcome tragic experiences. The transition can result in culture shock and lead to depression and a sense of isolation. Even though mass media enables populations to know more about each other than in earlier generations, people might also pick up misrepresentations that can result in greater culture clashes. Citizens and others in the receiving country might feel uncomfortable themselves dealing with incoming populations, exacerbating a difficult situation even more, rather than being open-minded enough to learn about other cultures and make appropriate adjustments or to offer help.

Literacy efforts may suffer too because of language differences, and the target country's educational system tends to favor instruction in its dominant language. Furthermore, those same educational institutions might have teachers who do not know how to deal with second-language learners. Indeed, education in general can be problematic for migrant populations because of first-country differences in practices and values. When migrating families have to focus on survival and acculturation, literacy education may take a back seat, even though it is a vital part of the acculturation process in finding and using social services (Constantino, 1998).

As an example of cross-cultural issues that affect literacy and the effect of technology, Lamsal (2014) studied the translingual and transcultural literacy practices of Bhutanese refugees in the United States. She noted the differences between U.S. citizens' view of Bhutanese/Nepalese cultures and the immigrants' actual situated practices. Lamsal also pointed out the distinction between voluntary and refugee immigrant populations, as well as the dynamics of intragroup differences (e.g., by caste, gender, or religion), relative to their literacy practices. Lamsal examined how the refugees used multilingual practices—especially through the use of new media—in globalized contexts and alternative language networks.

In researching cross-cultural e-learning, Edmundson (2007) developed a two-pronged approach in her cultural adaptation process (CAP) model of instructional design accommodation in order to address cultural differences between both the instructor and students as well as among the student population. One prong focuses on the learner; the other prong analyzes the course. Edmundson posits a four-step process, aligned with the complexity of the content.

AFGHANISTAN CENTER AT KABUL UNIVERSITY (ACKU)

The Afghanistan Center at Kabul University (ACKU) collects and preserves documents about Afghanistan and promotes literacy and academic research. Its ABLE (ACKU Box Library Extension) campaign was established in 1996 to improve the literacy skills of children and struggling adult readers. ABLE employs three strategies to meet this mission: it provides books to underserved areas and populations such as refugees, publishes and distributes locally written, easy-to-read books in Farsi-Dari and Pashto for children, and maintains a network of more than 270 libraries in thirty-four provinces, which they have established and updated over the years. Since its beginning, ABLE has benefitted more than half a million people in Afghanistan and Pakistan, even during the Taliban regime (Library of Congress, 2016).

1. Evaluate the content along a continuum, from simple, core information (such as basic procedures and products) to complex knowledge and soft skills (such as project management and conflict resolution).
2. Identify instructional methods and activities along the spectrum, from objectivist/rote to constructivist-cognitive/high-context communication.
3. Identify culturally contextualized learner preferences.
4. Provide adaptation strategies based on the above ascertainments.

For basic, objective learner outcomes in low-context cultural norms, materials just need to be translated with simple grammar and standard phrases. With increasing complexity and culture sensitivity, curricula need localization where resources and examples reflect the daily life and cultural context of the target learner. When cultural soft skills constitute the central learning outcome, then social norms need to be introduced with care and practiced in a safe environment, building on prior realities, as learners need to assimilate new cultural understandings (McMahon & Bruce, 2002).

At the least, as educators work with people from different cultures, they should strive for cultural competence and culturally responsive teaching (Kozleski, 2010). They can start by learning about the population they serve—their backgrounds, their interests, their needs, and their resources. Educators also need to confront their own cultural biases and do personal emotional work to improve their own mindset. They should be patient, empathetic, psychologically accessible, and open to new experiences (Craig, 1996). All learners should be able to access and understand curricula that bridge different ways of engagement and ways of knowing.

These same principles apply to all participants in educational experiences, with educators modeling appropriate behaviors. Mansilla and Jackson (2013) identified four indicators of globally culturally competent learners: investigating their extended world, recognizing and explaining different perspectives, communicating ideas effectively with diverse audiences, and taking action to improve conditions. Indeed, cross-cultural competence is a worthy goal of communities in general.

Focusing on migration experiences, several community-based literacy projects have incorporated cross-cultural and acculturation aspects into their approaches. In countries where many people have found refuge, public libraries have offered language "cafes" where language learners can practice conversations in the target language. Libraries also provide programming in mother tongues and hold workshops about navigating social services for incoming residents. All these efforts help immigrants build trust and social capital, which helps them belong to their new community (Vårheim, 2011).

Universities can play an important role in helping immigrants gain literacy skills. For example, university students training as TESOLs (teachers of English to speakers of other languages) tutored refugees as their service-learning project (Yang, 2015). The TESOLs developed intercultural competence through their teaching and social interactions with the refugees, and the learners also gained intercultural competence as well as English literacy and self-confidence.

In 2015, almost a million asylum applications were submitted in European countries, which challenged these countries as to how migrants could be integrated quickly. Recognizing the need for language acquisition and employment on an international scale, three universities and Macedonia's Community Development Institute developed culturally sensitive online resources to enhance the basic literacy and workplace skills of newly arrived adults. (Damiani & Agrusti, 2017).

Andrade and Doolin (2016) recognized the importance of social inclusion for newly resettled refugees. The researchers found that the use of ICT (information and communication technologies) facilitated refugees' communication, social connection, expression of cultural identity, understanding of the new community, and regaining control of their lives.

At a time when communities may see refugees as a threat or the influx of refugees as a burden or deficit, a participatory literacy project in immigrant communities is very welcome. Boston's programs for immigrants exemplifies this attitude (Auerbach et al., 2013). The local university trained educated immigrants in English as a second language. Outstanding trainees served as literacy mentors to train immigrants in turn, including family literacy. Because the trainers came from the immigrant communities, they understood newcomers' social problems and could advocate for them with existing local groups. More formally, community-based organizations shared their expertise and addressed concerns collaboratively. These efforts created jobs in the community, rather than taking jobs away; and they helped newcomers comply with local norms to facilitate smoother transitions—for example, immigrant mothers became more involved in their children's education. The programs were also successful because content was socially and culturally contextualized.

Overall, people gain cultural literacy as they interact across cultures in activities that are mutually meaningful. Basic literacy contributes significantly to this process because it facilitates communication. At the same time, literacy gains occur more rapidly and deeply when linked with other literacies, such as health and finance—skills needed for daily life.

The following resources provide valuable information about cultural literacy education.

American Library Association. *New Americans Library Project*. https://newamericans.ala.org/.

Asia-Pacific Centre of Education for International Understanding. *Global citizenship education: A guide for policymakers*. https://www.bridge47.org/sites/default/files/2018-12/global_citizenship_education_guide_for_policy_makers.pdf.

Calgary Board of Education. *Teaching refugees with limited formal schooling.* http://
teachingrefugees.com/.

Center for Global Studies. *Educational resources.* https://cgs.illinois.edu/global-e/
educational-resources/.

Childhood Education International. *Global education resources.* https://acei.org/
article/global-education-resources/.

Malaika Foundation. *Global educational resources and fellowships.* Central City, NE:
Malaika Foundation. http://www.malaikafoundation.org/development.html.

Participate Learning. *Global citizenship framework.* https://www.participatelearning
.com/global-education-resources/global-citizenship-framework/.

Ryan, G., & Flynn, A. (2017). *Action on global citizenship teacher toolkit.* Dublin,
Ireland: Global Action Plan. https://www.centreforglobaleducation.com/sites/
default/files/Action-on-Global-Citizenship.pdf.

School Library Journal. A diversity & cultural literacy toolkit. https://www.slj
.com/?detailStory=diversity-cultural-literacy-toolkit.

UNESCO. *Global citizenship education resources.* https://en.unesco.org/themes/gced/
resources.

UNESCO. *Selected publications and resources on global citizenship education and the
prevention of violent extremism through education.* https://conference.gene
.education/wp-content/uploads/UNESCO-GCED-Selected-publications-and
-resources.pdf.

REFERENCES

Abrahamson, J. A., Fisher, K. E., Turner, A. G., Durrance, J. C., & Turner, T. C. (2008).
Lay information mediary behavior uncovered: Exploring how nonprofessionals
seek health information for themselves and others online. *Journal of the Medical
Library Association, 96*(4), 310–323.

Andrade, A., & Doolin, B. (2016). Information and communication technology and
the social inclusion of refugees. *MIS Quarterly, 40*(2), 405–416.

Auerbach, E., Barahona, B., Midy, J., Vaquerano, F., Zambrano, A., & Arnaud, J.
(2013). *Adult ESL/literacy: From the community to the community: A guidebook for
participatory literacy training.* New York, NY: Routledge.

Brega A., Barnard, J., Mabachi, N., Weiss, B., DeWalt, D., Brach, C., Cifuentes, M.,
Albright, K., West, D. (2015). *AHRQ health literacy universal precautions toolkit*
(2nd ed.). Rockville, MD: Agency for Healthcare Research and Quality.

Burke, J., & Hughes-Hassell, S. (2007). Public library websites for teenagers: How
are they addressing the consumer health information needs of today's teens?
Proceedings of the American Society for Information Science and Technology, 44(1), 1–4.

Charmaraman, L. (2013). Congregating to create for social change: Urban youth
media production and sense of community. *Learning, Media and Technology,
38*(1), 102–115.

Coben, D., Dawes, M., & Lee, N. (2005). *Financial literacy education and 'Skills for Life': Research report.* London, UK: National Research and Development Centre.

Constantino, R. (Ed.). (1998). *Literacy, access, and libraries among the language minority population.* Lanham, MD: Scarecrow Press.

Council for Economic Education. (2013). *National standards for financial literacy.* New York, NY: Council for Economic Education.

Craig, R. (Ed.). (1996). *ASTD training and development handbook* (4th ed.). New York, NY: McGraw-Hill.

Crandall, H. (2016). Locating community action outreach projects in the scholarship of media literacy pedagogy. *Journal of Media Literacy Education, 8*(2), 110–121.

Crutzen, R. (2010). Strategies to facilitate exposure to internet-delivered health behavior change interventions aimed at adolescents or young adults: A systematic review. *Health Education and Behavior, 38*(1), 49–62.

Damiani, V., & Agrusti, G. (2017). Developing online resources for adult refugees in Italy: Foster skills that will enhance employability prospects. In *INTED2017 Proceedings* (pp. 5019–5027). Valencia, Spain: IATED.

Davis, J. (2014). *Library of Congress literacy awards 2014: Best practices.* Washington, DC: Library of Congress.

Davis, J. (2013). *Library of Congress literacy awards 2013: Best practices.* Washington, DC: Library of Congress.

Edmundson, A. (2007). The cultural adaptation process (CAP) model: Designing e-learning for another culture. In *Globalized e-learning cultural challenges* (pp. 267–290). Hershey, PA: IGI Global.

Fennell, R., & Escue, C. (2013). Using mobile health clinics to reach college students: A national demonstration project. *American Journal of Health Education, 44*(6), 343–348.

Fernandes, D., Lynch Jr., J. G., & Netemeyer, R. G. (2014). Financial literacy, financial education, and downstream financial behaviors. *Management Science, 60*(8), 1861–1883.

Freeny, M. (2013). *Library of Congress literacy awards 2013.* Washington, DC: Library of Congress.

Grauer, K., Castro, J. C., & Lin, C. C. (2012). Encounters with difference: Community-based new media programs and practices. *Studies in Art Education, 53*(2), 139–151.

Grizzle, A., Moore, P., Dezuanni, M., Asthana, S., Wilson, C., Banda, F., & Onumah, C. (2014). Media and information literacy: policy and strategy guidelines. Paris, France: UNESCO.

Hanemann, U., & UNESCO Institute for Lifelong Learning. (2015). *Transforming our world: Literacy for sustainable development.* Hamburg, Germany: UNESCO Institute for Lifelong Learning.

Harshman, J. (2017). Developing globally minded, critical media literacy skills. *Journal of Social Studies Education Research, 8*(1), 69–92.

Hobbs, R. (2013). Improvization and strategic risk-taking in informal learning with digital media literacy. *Learning, Media and Technology, 38*(2), 182–197.

Hobbs, R. (2010). *Digital and media literacy: A plan of action.* Washington, DC: Aspen Institute.

Kaya, V. H., & Elster, D. (2019). A critical consideration of environmental literacy: Concepts, contexts, and competencies. *Sustainability, 11*(6), 1581. doi:10.3390/su11061581

Kelly, K. (2012). Lack of training and a self-service environment leaves staff and users uncertain about health information in a public library setting. *Evidence Based Library and Information Practice, 7*(1), 122–124.

Kickbusch, I., Pelikan, J., Apfel, F., & Tsouros, A. (Eds.). (2013). *Health literacy.* Copenhagen, Denmark: World Health Organization.

Klapper, L., Lusardi, A., & van Oudheusden, P. (2015). *Financial literacy around the world.* Washington, DC: World Bank.

Kozleski, E. (2010). *Culturally responsive teaching matters!* Tempe, AZ: Equity Alliance.

Lamsal, T. R. (2014). *Globalizing literacies and identities: translingual and transcultural literacy practices of Bhutanese refugees in the US.* Doctoral dissertation, University of Louisville. Retrieved from https://doi.org/10.18297/etd/789.

Lariscy, R., Reber, B., & Paek, H. (2011). Exploration of health concerns and the role of social media information among rural and urban adolescents: A preliminary study. *International Electronic Journal of Health Education 14*,16–36.

Library of Congress. (2016). *Library of Congress literacy awards 2016.* Washington, DC: Library of Congress.

Mahasneh, R., Romanowski, M., & Dajani, R. (2017). Reading social stories in the community: A promising intervention for promoting children's environmental knowledge and behavior in Jordan. *Journal of Environmental Education, 48*(5), 334–346.

Mansilla, V., & Jackson, A. (2013). Educating for global competence: Learning redefined for an interconnected world. In H. Jacobs (Ed.), *Mastering global literacy: Contemporary perspectives* (pp. 5–30). New York, NY: Solution Tree.

McBride, B., Brewer, C., Berkowitz, A., & Borrie, W. (2013). Environmental literacy, ecological literacy, ecoliteracy: What do we mean and how did we get here? *Ecosphere, 4*(5), 1–20.

McMahon, C., & Bruce, C. (2002). Information literacy needs of local staff in cross-cultural development projects. *Journal of International Development, 14*(1), 113–137.

Muratova, N., & Grizzle, A. (2019). *Media and information literacy in journalism.* Paris, France: UNESCO.

National Association for Media Literacy Education. (2007). *Core principles of media literacy education in the United States*. New York, NY: National Association for Media Literacy Education.

North American Association for Environmental Education. (2011). *Environmental literacy framework*. Washington, DC: North American Association for Environmental Education.

Norris, E., & Osayande, E. (2017). Influence of adult literacy education on the environmental behaviours of women. *European Scientific Journal, 13*(20), 241–250.

Organisation for Economic Co-operation and Development. (2015). *National strategies for financial education*. Paris, France: Organisation for Economic Co-operation and Development.

Randall, T. (2019). *From food to thought: A path to ecoliteracy in higher education*. Doctoral dissertation, University of California, Los Angeles. Available from ProQuest Dissertations and Theses database (UMI no. 22622691).

Reference and User Services Association. (2014). *Financial literacy education in libraries: Guidelines and best practices for service*. Chicago, IL: American Library Association.

Reynolds, H., Brondizio, E., Robinson, J. (Eds.). (2010). *Teaching environmental literacy: Across campus and across the curriculum*. Bloomington, IN: Indiana University Press.

Scholz, R., & Gallati, J. (2011). *Environmental literacy in science and society: From knowledge to decisions*. Cambridge, MA: Cambridge University Press.

Silverblatt, A., Ferry, J., & Finan, B. (2015). *Approaches to media literacy*. New York, NY: Routledge.

Sorensen, K., et al. (2012). Health literacy and public health: A systematic review and integration of definitions and models. *BMC Public Health, 12,* 80. Retrieved from https://bmcpublichealth.biomedcentral.com/articles/10.1186/1471-2458-12-80.

UNESCO. (2002). *Universal Declaration on Cultural Diversity*. Paris, France: UNESCO.

UNESCO Institute for Lifelong Learning. (2016). *Promoting health and literacy for women's empowerment*. Hamburg, Germany: UNESCO Institute for Lifelong Learning.

U.S. Department of Health and Human Services. Office of Disease Prevention and Health Promotion. (2010). *Quick guide to health literacy*. Washington, DC: Government Printing Office.

U.S. Financial Literacy and Education Commission. (2019). *Best practices for financial literacy and education at institutions of higher education*. Washington, DC: U.S. Financial Literacy and Education Commission.

U.S. Office of Disease Prevention and Health Promotion. (2019). *Educational and community-based programs*. Washington, DC: U.S. Office of Disease Prevention and Health Promotion. Retrieved from http://healthyPeople.gov.

Varela-Losada, M., Vega-Marcote, P., Pérez-Rodríguez, U., & Álvarez-Lires, M. (2016). Going to action? A literature review on educational proposals in formal Environmental Education. *Environmental Education Research*, *22*(3), 390–421.

Vårheim, A. (2011). Gracious space: Library programming strategies towards immigrants as tools in the creation of social capital. *Library & Information Science Research,* *33*(1), 12–18.

Willis, L. E. (2013). Financial education: Lessons not learned & lessons learned. *Life-Cycle Investing: Financial Education and Consumer Protection*, *125*. Retrieved from http://dx.doi.org/10.2139/ssrn.1869313.

Yang, P. (2015). Developing intercultural competence in TESOL service-learning: Volunteer tutoring for recently-arrived adult refugees in learning English as a second language. In J. Perren & A. Wurr (Eds.), *Learning the language of global citizenship: Strengthening service-learning in TESOL* (pp. 331–354). Champaign, IL: Common Ground.

6

Planning Literacy Projects

The case for literacy is strong. The community need for literacy is strong (if for no other reason than children are born every year). The challenge is meeting that need for literacy in an effective manner. This chapter provides a framework of action research, and then details the typical steps in planning and implementing effective literacy projects.

ACTION RESEARCH

Action research provides a useful framework to couch literacy projects (Schutz & Hoffman, 2017). The concept that underlies action research is a systematic approach to addressing and positively resolving an issue. In the arena of literacy, action research identifies the literacy problem, determines the underlying factors that contribute to the literacy problem, suggests ways to solve the literacy problem, creates interventions to solve that problem, and then assesses the effectiveness of those interventions.

Action research differs from formal research. First, it is participatory—the researchers are part of the system, not outsiders. While they might be less objective, they have inside information and so are better positioned to identify and solve an issue. Second, action research is action-oriented—it is practical, and it is grounded in the hope of successful outcomes. Third, because the issue and solution depend on the specific situation and context, the action might not work in another situation, unlike the intent of most formal research.

On the other hand, action research follows a systematic process, as listed here. An example for each step follows.

1. *Focus on a need or topic.* A school administrator called a meeting with a school parent volunteer, service club officer, mayor, religious leader, and librarian. The group thought that children seemed to be losing reading competency over the summer when school was out. To show their commitment to the issue, the participants established group roles and procedures, including a communications plan.

2. *Review and synthesize research on the topic.* The librarian took the lead on researching the issue. Research stated that reading during the summer does mitigate the "summer slide." The slide mostly affects children in lower-socioeconomic families, and those children benefit the most from summer reading—and dramatically reduces achievement gaps between high- and low-income peers. Several successful summer reading programs were found and reviewed; key factors included access to books, freedom to choose what to read, adult encouragement and modeling, making reading fun, sharing reading experiences, reading four to six books as a goal, collaborating as community organizations. Great websites were found, such as National Summer Learning Organization (https://www.summerlearning.org/)and Summermatters.net.

3. *Develop research questions.* What community-wide summer reading effort focused on children might mitigate reading competency loss over the summer?

4. *Collect data.* The steering group collected end-of-year and beginning-of-year reading scores, library summer reading statistics (e.g., number of participants, participant demographics, community map showing public places, number of books read), and a family survey of summer reading practices (a good survey tool was found).

5. *Analyze data.* The biggest drop in reading occurred among older elementary children (9- and 10-year-olds), boys more than girls. Families who read more had more books at home or visited the library. Families who read less shared reading less. Over 95 percent of families had cell phones. All families were within one mile of a shopping area, school, religious center, community center, or park. Reasons for not reading more included lack of awareness, other things to do, and lack of convenient reading material.

6. *Report results.* The analysis was written by the mayor's office and edited by the steering group. Based on the analyzed data, the group decided to focus on increasing summer reading for 9- and 10-year-olds. Their

strategies included increasing access to reading material and providing convenient public venues for shared reading. The group also identified available resources to ensure that they could carry out a summer reading plan. They further identified feasible public indoor and outdoor spaces; possible sources of reading materials; volunteer groups that could collect, store and disseminate reading materials; volunteer groups that could facilitate reading events; persons who could manage communications; persons who could coordinate logistics; and possible sources of funding as needed. The group also developed a beginning timetable. Each person in the group disseminated the information to their network with the idea of brainstorming ways to make the goal operational. The steering group also decided to ask one person in their network to join the steering group to add representation and expertise.

7. *Design an action plan based on the data.* Based on the input of the community groups, the group decided to institute two public places each day to read, at two times, focusing on available parks and parking lots. They would gather books and other reading materials to take and share. They would also create a Facebook page and a Twitter feed so families could access online reading materials and share their reading experiences online. The steering group came up with the project name: Park, Pick and Read. The group then developed an action team to visualize the action plan, noting the following: the overall task, target groups, person or personnel responsible, resources, benchmarks, time frame, and evidence-based assessment. Each aspect required detailed tasks—for instance, collecting reading materials involved defining what material was appropriate, who had appropriate materials, who could contact the source for the materials, who would collect them and when, where the materials would be stored, who would review the collected materials for appropriateness and physical condition, how sets of duplicate items could be created and stored, how items would be disseminated and collected at the event—and by whom. Even details such as checking on permits for group events, first aid and security measures, seating options, and food options, had to be considered and addressed. As much as possible, the planners leveraged their prior experience and available summer reading plan documents from successful programs.

8. *Take action.* The steering group provided oversight of the action team's implementation. To that end, the steering group trained the team as needed, monitored and redirected their performance as needed, and rewarded them for their successful efforts. To test the idea, the school did a trial run during spring break in the school parking lot using the steering group, the action team, a parent group, and available teachers as

facilitators. The result was a modest success, and follow-up surveys and volunteer debriefing provided useful feedback to refine the project.

9. *Evaluate the action.* Both the plan process and results were assessed before, during and after the summer project. Corrections and modifications were done as needed, making sure that any changes were reviewed, approved, and well communicated.

UNESCO's Institute for Lifelong Learning has worked with many organizations of literacy action research projects. Examples of their current activities are located at http://uil.unesco.org/literacy/action-research.

STARTING WITH PLANNERS

Literacy improvement is a constant goal. Each new generation marks a new opportunity to ensure literacy for all. How each community deals with literacy is unique—and dynamic. While literacy projects can impact readers at the family or classroom level, literacy projects with larger audiences can offer a greater capacity for effective and efficient literacy gains. Such efforts require partnerships to build that capacity through expanded and complementary resources and expertise. Furthermore, community partnerships can reinforce and support literacy efforts across various settings.

Even before the search for partners, the initial group needs to identify a possible goal based on their informed perspective of a literacy situation in the community. What is happening now, and what would they like to see happen? Perhaps employers are complaining that their employees can't read company documents. Perhaps schools are complaining that first graders have no sense of the alphabet. Perhaps elders want to have more opportunities to tell stories. These initial needs can prime the literacy project pump. The more specific and comprehensive the data, the easier it will be to identify goals and potential partners to help achieve those goals.

Identifying Partners

Therefore, one of the first tasks in planning literacy projects is identifying, recruiting, and involving partners (Smallwood, 2010). Stakeholders are the most obvious choice because they are impacted by literacy. Each potential partner has potential expertise, resources, services, and networks that can contribute to the literacy effort. The originating group can model that list of assets in light of literacy. For instance, libraries exemplify community-based service that supports literacy. They build and maintain rich collections of literacy materials that are freely available to the entire community at hopefully convenient hours in welcoming facilities. Libraries are staffed by trained personnel who know how to provide physical and intellectual access to those literacy materials.

Nevertheless, establishing partnerships can be challenging. Some groups do not want to partner because they do not see the benefit, especially if they think that they are giving away more than they are getting. Everyone has to benefit for a partnership to develop and continue. While a one-time effort might be more acceptable, it does not develop commitment and could negate long-term benefits. To be fair, partnerships take time and effort, and can slow down processes. Leadership has to be negotiated and shared. Any benefits have to outweigh those challenges. Ideally, those benefits can include improved public relations, increased demand for services, greater participation in the entity's enterprise, access to more literacy resources and expertise, and the bottom line: improved literacy. Being forthcoming about benefits and challenges can help coming to agreement.

What information, then, should be gathered about potential partnerships? Each question should be considered in light of literacy.

- What is the potential partner's mission?
- What is their background?
- What experience and expertise do they bring?
- What is their staffing?
- What are their resources?
- What is their financial status, including revenue and expenses?
- What is their governance structure and leadership style?
- Who do they influence in terms of literacy, and how is that accomplished?
- What are their literacy interests and needs?
- What are their expectations and hopes?
- What are they willing to share and commit to?
- How do they want to partner?

This information about each group helps configure how partners will work with each other to optimize efforts and results. It is also the start of developing a relationship that can build on mutual respect and trust.

Ideally, the initial team should consist of six to a dozen key stakeholder representatives. Even at this point, the team members should be associated with some group, and they should have strong influence or networking contacts. That number of people has enough different points of view to avoid groupthink and provides enough resources among them to establish a substantial literacy project. It should be understood that this team does not yet constitute a true partnership; the team might decide not to proceed. However, this first team provides enough input to determine if an action plan is worth spending the time to develop and implement. Moreover, the team together serves as a powerful, increasingly cohesive sign that can attract and recruit other relevant partners.

Even at this early point in team formation, the group has to recognize the value of each member, clarify roles, and select team leaders. They also need to develop a communication system: creating a contact directory, setting up a meeting schedule, establishing a storage mechanism for documents, creating social media pages as needed, establishing communication mechanisms between meetings, and developing a public relations plan (Epstein et al., 2018).

BRING ME A BOOK

Bring Me a Book is a volunteer-based nonprofit organization that supports school and reading readiness through access to books. The power of their program lies in their effective use of broad-based partnerships. From the beginning, they have given away children's books to under-resourced families through partner schools, clinics, and other nonprofit organizations. The books are chosen through partnerships with children's literature experts; service clubs and other donors underwrite the books; and volunteers process them. Book cubbies complement the book giveaways: families participate in literacy education and are given these cubbies to use to hold their children's home library. Book buddies consist of trained volunteers who commit one year to read aloud to students and give books to the children and classroom libraries. The program, which started in San Francisco, has spread to Southern California, Missouri, Florida, and Hong Kong (Library of Congress, 2016).

PRELIMINARY PLANNING

With an initial team in place, the following groundwork can provide the basis for the ultimate action plan.

Needs Assessment

The next step for the initial team is to clarify the literacy situation to determine the group's literacy goals and objectives. To this end, the group should conduct a needs assessment: What are literacy practices and results now, and what needs to happen to improve literacy? (Sleezer, Russ-Eft, & Gupta, 2014). Unless a clear mandate has already been set, the team can cast a wide net to discern patterns and trends in their community. For instance, they may see high unemployment due to illiteracy, low educational retention and graduation rates, ineffective reading instruction in early grades, and low educational achievement among parents. Inadequate literacy training in this situation is systemic. The team should also assess the preconditions for this situation: publishing, access to reading materials, opportunities for learning and practicing literacy, and preparation of literacy teachers. Then they must prioritize their goals in terms of the most demanding need, the availability of resources and expertise, and the greatest return on investment. A second needs assessment may be called for in order to dig deeper into a more defined and narrower scope, such as reaching families.

Gathering data about a community's literacy situation typically involves a number of strategies: surveys, focus groups, interviews, observations, and document analysis. The initial team should probably start with existing data and then identify data gaps so that targeted data collection can be done efficiently. Already, the need for efficient documentation, organization, and storage becomes clear. Moreover, the initial team needs available expertise to analyze the data effectively.

Goals and Objectives

The initial analysis can jumpstart the identification of data-based goals and objectives, bridging the gap between the current situation and the desired outcome. However, those goals and certainly the objectives also have to be considered alongside the available resources, services, and expertise that can lead to the desired outcome. Therefore, the team should also inventory those factors that can contribute to achieving the tentative goal. For instance, if the team decides to focus on family literacy, they have to find out what reading materials for children and for parents are available. If the team wants to include digital materials, they have to determine the state of internet connectivity and the number of families having internet-connected devices. They also have to find out who is available to train parents in early literacy skills as well as incorporate reading skills training for adult learners. Are there sufficient volunteers available to be trained by an expert in order to scale up the family literacy efforts? What added resources are needed, and how can they be acquired? As the team balances needs with resources, they can refine their goals and objectives to result in a feasible plan.

Generally, goals express intended results or outcomes in brief statements, and they reflect core values and longer-term visions. Objectives provide concrete strategies to reach the goals. Objectives should be SMART: specific, measurable, attainable, relevant, and time-bound. To be effective, most literacy projects should focus on just a couple of goals in order to marshal resources and personnel effectively. Likewise, each goal should have only a handful of objectives. The initial team might well have more goals and objectives to begin with, but they should prioritize those goals and objectives to avoid a scattered effort—which objectives and their activities will offer the greatest impact for the effort? Furthermore, additional objectives might emerge later, so it is better to start with a focused plan and build on success.

TABLE 6.1

Action-Plan Template

Goal:									
Result/Outcome:				Result/Outcome Measurement:					
Objective	Target Audience	Activity	Content	Resources	Personnel	Support	Time Frame	Assessment

Charting goals and objectives helps clarify them for the planners and aids in communicating them to other stakeholders. Table 6.1 may be used as a template to guide the charting process.

At this point, the specifics for meeting the team objectives might be brainstormed but not decided on. External facts and guidance are needed.

Literature Review

What impactful practices have other literacy projects implemented? What possible theories might apply to an identified literacy effort? Professional associations and trade publications can provide valuable information that can optimize literacy efforts. For instance, a literature review can reveal the underlying factors of a particular literacy issue and the validated assessment instruments to measure those factors. A literature review can also identify methods to resolve that issue as well as discusses ineffective strategies. Furthermore, a literature review can identify experts who might possibly provide guidance for the literacy project.

As inspirational as some literacy research may be, their contexts must also be considered. Ideally, the closer the match between the research's population, environment, resources, personnel, situation, and literacy issue with that of the projected literacy effort, the greater the likelihood that the assessments and solutions can be applied to the literacy goals at hand. Therefore, any literature review needs to be examined closely. Overall, though, culling from the relevant literature can inform the ultimate action plan, such as factors contributing to the lack of literacy, training tools, or assessment instruments. The chart template above (table 6.1) can serve as a guide to extract applicable factors.

LIBRARIES WITHOUT BORDERS

Libraries Without Borders (LWB) brings resources and knowledge tools to areas of need, from refugee camps to post-disaster sites in fifty countries. Their signature product is the Ideas Box: a "pop-up" media center with reading materials, board games, cameras, internet-connected laptops and tablets preloaded with relevant digital content, one large-monitor screen, one electric generator, and furniture. The Ideas Box is stored in four metal boxes that fit on two pallets and can be set up in twenty minutes. Before the box is assembled, each potential community is assessed in order to provide relevant materials. Local volunteers are trained to maintain the media center, and LWB monitors and supports their efforts (Library of Congress, 2016).

ACTION PLAN

Informed with an understanding of the literacy need, using internal data coupled with the literature, the initial team is ready to create the actual action plan. At this point, the initial team may configure an action-plan team, comprised of both some initial team members and new individuals and groups. While the initial team envisioned the big picture, the action-plan team focuses on the details of the objectives' implementation. Again, the core action-plan team should probably include six to twelve members. In most cases, again, those members represent partner groups, but they may come from new partners that have been identified by the initial team as being critically important to the literacy project's outcome. For instance, the action-plan team might include a comptroller, an effective manager, and a communications expert. Each objective might have a point person heading a subcommittee made up of specialists. Most likely, the initial team and action-plan team will collaboratively create the outline of the action plan.

First, the action-plan team has to organize itself, including selecting their leader and full-time coordinator. They need to develop their communication plan and other coordinating activities, just as the initial team had to do. Some activities require joint responsibility, such as recruitment, management, and coordination. Other roles may be better handled individually or by a subcommittee, such as a liaison for a partner.

Logistics constitutes a major part of action-plan team's efforts. For that reason, that team needs to set agreements for how they participate and how each partner operates. A written agreement spelling out specific expectations is a wise practice. Furthermore, those partners need to collaborate to some extent, which means that the action-plan team needs to facilitate those interactions as well. In the process, the team also has to determine what additional resources might be needed in order to implement the plan. It should be noted that the team is not alone; they can ask their partners for help with those logistics. The action-plan team also has to realize that they may need to make adjustments in their plan as they assess how the implementation is working. The key consideration, though, is the target learner population.

Audience

Literacy projects focus on the audience—not only the primary ones, who are gaining literacy skills, but also those secondary audiences who either benefit from the literacy gains (such as classroom teachers or employers) or those who are supporting the literacy effort (such as parents or tutors). The action-plan team needs to determine the roles for each audience, and then the supporting resources and services for each audience.

As an early step, the action-plan team must determine effective ways to contact the target audience—usually through relevant partners such as schools, workplace, religious centers, or other social groups—in order to know about them and recruit them efficiently. A communications plan will determine:

- the method of communication: oral, written, visual
- the communications channel: word of mouth, parent newsletter, church bulletin, social media
- the communication style: formal, informal, FAQs
- language: English, home language

While the core goal and message should be consistent, each audience sector needs a customized approach.

How will the audience be supported? The action-plan team needs to understand the audience's characteristics, environment, and situation as it considers the preconditions and support needed for audience participation. How will participants get to the literacy site? Should transportation be provided? What timing is most convenient? Is food needed? Is childcare needed? The target participants need to know that they are supported, and that the benefits are worth any possible inconveniences or challenges.

Content

Based on the target audience and their literacy needs, the action-plan team can work with literacy experts to determine the literacy content and curriculum (Wiles, 2004).

- What are the learners' needed literacy skills?
- What are the learners' current literacy conditions and situations?
- How does the audience's culture impact the curriculum?
- What content interests and engages the learners?
- What literacy materials are relevant and available?
- What language should be used for content matter and instruction?

- What delivery structure is used: workshops, classroom instruction, one-to-one coaching, online tutorials, and so on?
- What is the time frame: length of the interaction, length of each event, timing of each event, timing with other associated events, synchronous or asynchronous?
- What are the locations of the literacy activity: public or private, indoors or outdoors, facilities and their features, furniture and its arrangement, available technology?
- What are the learning activities?
- What measurements are used to assess learning, delivery, processes, and planning?

The curriculum needs to address each target audience. For instance, if the objective is family literacy, then adult needs should be considered as well as children's needs. In some cases, the curriculum is shared with both parties, and in other cases, a secondary-party curriculum might complement the target learners' literacy curriculum.

Personnel

Several kinds of people are needed to implement literacy projects: curriculum designers and deliverers, trainers, organizers, clerical staff, communicators, assessors, fiscal agents. Each goal and its associated objectives need to identify the relevant personnel. These people may be paid or volunteers, experts, or willing learners. Just as with the target audience, support personnel need to be brought on board, trained, monitored, and assessed.

To assemble the appropriate personnel, the action-plan team—with the help of function-specific experts—should develop job descriptions, qualifications, and criteria for hiring them. In addition, developing and using volunteer forms and interview protocols ensure an equitable process and a better probability of matching personnel with literacy functions. The forms also help provide clear information for targeted recruitment communication. Regardless of the function, recruiters should help new personnel realize the significance of their role in achieving literacy goals.

Literacy partners can use these forms, especially as they provide the most probable sources of personnel. In collaboration with the action-plan team, partners can help recruit, interview, train, and even monitor personnel. Just as literacy partners contribute to and help validate literacy projects, their role in dealing with literacy-project personnel can facilitate the socialization and assimilation of those personnel.

Once brought onto the project, personnel often need training; interviews and recommendations can help determine what training is needed. Even function-specific experts should demonstrate their ability and may need assimilation into the literacy project if appropriate. As with recruitment, training should include curricula, processes, and protocols to ensure consistent skills and knowledge. Regardless of the function, training usually involves demonstrating how to do the task, sharing relevant policies and procedures, talking through the task with the procedures in hand, reviewing the task and clarifying any aspects, observing and correcting the person's independent work, and monitoring the person's performance to ensure quality and consistency. Training should also consider the trainees' personal and cultural factors, just as literacy instructors try to align the curriculum with learners' factors.

The action-plan team should pay special attention to volunteer personnel. These individuals give of their time and effort for several possible reasons: interest in literacy, belief in the project, opportunity to gain skills, career exploration, sense of belonging, opportunity to socialize and network, community involvement and service, and school credit. Volunteers can technically quit anytime, so their commitment is especially important to obtain. Socialization and team-building constitute important components of volunteer work. Similarly, although all personnel appreciate recognition of a job well done, volunteers especially merit such thanks.

ROOM TO READ

Room to Read's mission is to create lifelong, independent readers. To that end, they work with local communities and donors to establish school libraries and distribute culturally relevant books to under-resourced schools. They also train teachers in literacy skills instruction and library management. To increase their impact, Room to Read invests in publishing local-language books for children and area businesses. As of 2020, more than eighteen million children at more than 3,500 sites have benefited from this program (Davis, 2014).

IMPLEMENTATION

All the factors discussed above are part of the action plan and its implementation. The plan sets up the structure and the resources, and the personnel act on those resources within the structure. The action-plan team manages and oversees that implementation to ensure that it enables the objectives and the goals to be met effectively with the ultimate outcome of improved literacy.

Management consists largely of assessing the implementation systematically: assessing each input, each activity, and its impact on the other inputs and actions to achieve the desired output. Assessment leads the manager to make adjustments through coaching personnel and adjusting resources as needed to redirect performance. For large literacy projects, several managers or supervisors are needed, with an overarching coordinating leader.

Throughout implementation, the action-plan team and managers should consult their project chart, built on their action plan. From the start, they should identify milestones to measure their progress and success, which can help them celebrate and recalibrate efforts. They should also document their work along the way: a paper or digital trail that can be used to assess planning and implementation.

MANGO TREE

The company Mango Tree started in 2000 as a response to the revision of the Leblango orthography in northern Uganda. Local education systems partner with Mango Tree to create low-cost, culturally appropriate educational materials in the mother tongue for primary school children and training guides for teachers. The community monitors and supports this literacy education to ensure quality instructional and literacy achievement that fosters a culture of reading (Lamolinara, 2018).

COMMUNICATION AND PUBLIC RELATIONS

To be impactful, literacy projects require regular and effective communication within and across each sector as well as to the community. The literacy project needs to be explained to its planners and implementers, partners, stakeholders, and the community at large in order to create awareness, interest, and support. The project's progress and results should be shared with affected personnel in order to sustain and improve performance, and the project's successful impact should be widely celebrated to recognize efforts and build community pride.

While communication takes place continuously, the literacy project action-plan team should also develop a strategic and systematic plan for communicating in order to allocate staff and resources predictably, as well as to optimize project impact. For instance, a literacy project may offer a story-hour series and summer reading program, which can be planned and scheduled in order to advertise them for maximum, predictable participation. Starting new literacy services—such as family literacy programs—needs special attention to communications planning to help make the community aware of this new offering.

Communications as an action-plan management function may be considered in light of a communications planning model (University of Kansas, 2018):

- Determine the purpose, such as fostering news literacy.
- Identify the target audience, such as secondary school teachers.
- Plan and design the message, such as teaching strategies for evaluating a news source communicated through a workshop, poster, or online tutorial.
- Consider available resources, such as knowledgeable and available trainers, news articles, computers, and handouts.
- Plan for obstacles and emergencies, such as printing out articles when internet access isn't available.
- Strategize how to connect with others, such as youth-serving agencies, to spread the message.
- Create an action plan, such as a professional development workshop for secondary school teachers.
- Evaluate the effectiveness of planning and teaching, follow-up choice, and use of news sources—for example, the degree and quality of teacher participation.

The more-general interaction and strategic communication between the literacy project and the community are defined as public relations (PR). Some aspects of PR include:

- Promotion: communicating the literacy project's value to the community
- Marketing: matching the community's needs and interests with the literacy project's resources and services
- Advocacy: developing understanding and support from decision-makers for community improvement

Some ways that a literacy project advances its public relations include:

- Good service: the best public relations of all
- Effective programming, such as visiting authors, storytelling, workshops, contests
- Literacy project web portal and social media
- Physical promotions, such as signs, posters, displays, bookmarks
- Publications, such as newsletters, newspaper articles, multimedia, social media
- Outreach actions, such as participating in community groups and events
- Recruitment
- Assessment efforts, such as surveys and focus groups

The ultimate goal of communication is to build literacy-based relationships. By establishing and nurturing meaningful professional relationships through effective communication and action, literacy projects build a stronger and broader support base and can improve literacy and overall community development.

> ## BEANSTALK
>
> Beanstalk is a national volunteer-based literacy charter that provides one-on-one tutoring for struggling readers ages 6 to 11, mainly in low socioeconomic areas. Volunteers are trained in literacy practices that engage students, and they are meeting with their assigned students twice a week for the entire school year. To raise awareness of the importance of reading and literacy and garner more public support for literacy efforts, Beanstalk partnered with the *London Evening Standard* to write and publish articles about the state of children's literacy and the consequences of illiteracy. Their Get London Reading campaign resulted in a national project to help children with literacy problems. More recently, Beanstalk launched a social platform to share ideas about literacy activities for children with their families (Davis, 2015).

CONTINUOUS ASSESSMENT AND IMPROVEMENT

Assessment plays a vital role, beginning with a literacy project's vision through its end and debriefing. Assessment sets the bar for expected achievement of meeting goals and objectives. It provides the data to examine the quality of actions and their results. It provides guidelines for capacity and performance. Assessment even helps systemize fiscal management. Each resource and action, and their interaction, should be assessed, analyzed, and acted on in order to optimize the literacy project's impact.

Different types of evaluation have different objectives and ask different questions:

- Needs assessments describe the current situation, identify gaps, and determine what is needed to fill those gaps.
- Process evaluation examines the way projects are planned and implemented.
- Formative evaluation measures progress and examines how to improve efforts along the way.
- Summative evaluation measures the ultimate success of an effort.

Several examples of assessment have already been mentioned in this chapter: from needs assessment surveys to job descriptions, from inventorying resources to evaluating literacy materials, from determining partnerships to determining project impact. Whenever possible, project teams should use existing validated assessment tools, which provide a useful guide and can still be customized to reflect unique aspects of the community involved.

Assessments occur at every level of literacy projects: from a single read-aloud fluency assessment to a yearly reading program review, from a volunteer coaching session to a partnership evaluation, from a software evaluation to a curriculum review. Both process and product should be assessed, since one influences the other.

Regardless of the assessment, the data collection process itself involves addressing several questions:

- Who is evaluating? Who is collecting the data? Who is organizing the data that is collected?
- How is the data collection being conducted?
- When is the data collection done—at the start of an effort, the middle, or the end? What is the data collection's time period? How frequently is data collection conducted?
- Where is the data collection done—at home, in a public space, face-to-face, online?

Here are representative systems of assessment:

Colorado Assessment Literacy Program. https://www.cde.state.co.us/assessment/coassessmentlitprog.

Foster, G. (2008). Literacy program assessment checklist. In *Working together to improve literacy* (pp. 26–28). Markham, Ontario: Pembroke Publishers. https://www.pembrokepublishers.com/data/ff/Program%20Assessment.pdf.

International Literacy Association standards. https://www.literacyworldwide.org/get-resources/standards.

Irvin, J., Meltzer, J., & Dukes, M. (2007). Chapter 5. Develop and implement a schoolwide literacy action plan. In *Taking action on adolescent literacy* (pp. 117–143). Alexandria, VA: ASCD. http://www.ascd.org/publications/books/107034/chapters/Develop-and-Implement-a-Schoolwide-Literacy-Action-Plan.aspx.

Joint Task Force on Assessment of the International Reading Association and the National Council of Teachers of English. (2010). *Standards for the assessment of reading and writing* (Rev. ed.). Newark, DE. https://www.literacyworldwide.org/docs/default-source/resource-documents/standards-for-the-assessment-of-reading-and-writing.pdf.

National Center for Education Statistics. (2016). *National assessment of adult literacy*. Washington, DC: National Center for Education Statistics. https://nces.ed.gov/naal/.

Southern and Eastern Africa Consortium for Monitoring Educational Quality. http://www.iiep.unesco.org/en/our-expertise/sacmeq.

Trawick, A. (2017). *Using the PIAAC literacy framework to guide instruction: An introduction for adult educators*. Washington, DC: U.S. Department of Education. https://static1.squarespace.com/static/51bb74b8e4b0139570ddf020/t/588b98bba5790a5bdd26679d/1485543612832/Literacy_Guide_Trawick_2017.pdf.

UNESCO. (2019). *Global education monitoring report*. Paris, France: UNESCO. https://en.unesco.org/gem-report/.

UNESCO. (2015). *RAMAA (Action Research: Measuring Literacy Program Participants' Learning Outcomes)*. Paris, France: UNESCO. http://uil.unesco.org/literacy/ measurement-of-learning-outcomes-ramaa.

UNESCO Institute for Statistics. (2016). *Literacy assessment and monitoring programme (LAMP)*. Paris, France: UNESCO. http://uis.unesco.org/sites/default/ files/documents/literacy-assessment-and-monitoring-programme-lamp -information-brochure-en.pdf.

Data's value depends on its analysis, and the analysis is only as good as the quality of the data. Therefore, before data can be analyzed, it has to be:

- Organized: into a spreadsheet, categorically, chronologically, etc.
- Cleaned up: of typos, missing data, illogical data (e.g., open eight days a week)
- Coded: normalizing data such as changing words into numbers (e.g., Monday = 1, Tuesday = 2, and so forth) for easier analysis

Only then can the action-plan team see the trends and patterns of the data clearly and accurately.

When analyzing assessment data, the action-plan team and other leaders should look for patterns and trends over time. Several analysis methods exist, and should align with data collection. Typically, qualitative data methods such as interviews and observations are coded for recurring themes or patterns. Quantitative data such as circulation records or attendance counts lend themselves to statistical analysis methods. Descriptive statistics can identify the range and distribution of values, the degree of homogeneity, and possible outlying values. Inferential statistics can identify possible relationships between factors, such as number of pages read and reading fluency. Visualizations of data can clarify patterns in data, facilitating their analysis and reporting. Nevertheless, statistics are not the answer; the team has to find the reason, the basis, for the patterns. Here are some questions to ask when beginning to analyze data (Connaway, 2017):

- Are some observations or responses overwhelmingly the same, such as the need for more materials in the home language?
- What kinds of trends do you see over time—growth, decline, clustering?
- Is there a big difference at some point in a trend, such as a dip in participation around holidays or a peak in tutoring services before final exams?
- What factors seem to stand out from the rest in terms of trends? Maybe one staff person's output differs from the rest.
- Does there seem to be a relationship between two factors, such as age and time of day of library visits?
- How do the data compare to another community's or to national literacy trends?

- How many people or observations are involved? If the number is small—say, less than fifty—then it will be harder to see a pattern that can be generalized or for which you can do inferential statistics.

Once the data from those assessments are analyzed, the action-plan team and other leaders can make decisions and act on them. For instance, when assessment is used to improve procedures, the manager can use the data as the driver for group analysis to solve problems together. The conclusions from those assessments should be shared with the affected stakeholders to inform them and to serve as input for future direction. Such communication also demonstrates that the literacy project is community-centered, listening to the community and caring enough to improve their literacy experience.

REFERENCES

Connaway, L. (2017). *Research methods in library and information science*. Santa Barbara, CA: Libraries Unlimited.

Davis, J. (2015). *Library of Congress literacy awards 2015: Best practices*. Washington, DC: Library of Congress.

Davis, J. (2014). *Library of Congress literacy awards 2014: Best practices*. Washington, DC: Library of Congress.

Epstein, J., et al. (2018). *School, family, and community partnerships* (4th ed.). Thousand Oaks, CA: Corwin.

Lamolinara, G. (2018). *Library of Congress literacy awards 2018*. Washington, DC: Library of Congress.

Library of Congress. (2016). *Library of Congress literacy awards 2016*. Washington, DC: Library of Congress.

Schutz, K., & Hoffman, J. (2017). "I practice teaching": Transforming our professional identities as literacy teachers through action research. *The Reading Teacher, 71*(1), 7–12.

Sleezer, C., Russ-Eft, D., & Gupta, K. (2014). *A practical guide to needs assessment* (3rd ed.). New York, NY: Pfeiffer.

Smallwood, C. (2010). *Librarians as community partners: An outreach handbook*. Chicago, IL: American Library Association.

University of Kansas. Center for Community Health and Development. (2018). *Community tool box*. Lawrenceville, KS: University of Kansas. https://ctb.ku.edu/en.

Wiles, J. (2004). *Curriculum essentials* (2nd ed.). Boston, MA: Allyn & Bacon.

Next Steps

Literacy needs always exist. Every time a baby is born, a literacy need is also born. Older people may have literacy needs because they did not have opportunities for schooling when they were growing up. People migrating from one country to another may well have literacy issues, if for no other reason than literacy is needed to navigate social services and employment bureaucracy. People with physical and mental differences such as deafness or cognitive delays may have literacy challenges. Some literacy needs may arise from cultural norms that prefer oral language to written text or to cultures that do not value females' education. In other cases, accidents or disease may result in people learning how to read in different ways, such as non-natal blindness.

Furthermore, different levels of literacy exist. One might be able to read simple text but not decipher legalese or complex texts. Each profession has its own specialized vocabulary and writing style, which may challenge the functionally literate. The writing side of literacy can also stump people who have not mastered academic writing or have physical limitations.

How can community members collaborate to address these literacy needs? How do they build capacity?

First, communities should inventory their own literacy resources. This task is likely to be done by major literacy constituents such as government officials, literacy-related organizational leaders, and educators. Typical literacy resource inventory questions follow.

- Who is literate? Who can teach literacy? Who can tutor someone to gain literacy competence? What is the quality of their expertise? How available are literacy experts? What are their associated costs?
- Who are literacy stakeholders, such as families, employers, businesses, health professionals, government agencies, religious leaders, media outlets? How does literacy impact them? What literacy expertise do they have? What support do they lend to literacy efforts? What is the quality of their support? How are decisions made concerning resource allocation and participation?
- What literacy education is available? What is its quality? Who has access to education? What is the basis for access? What costs are associated with access to literacy education? What policies exist relative to literacy education?
- What spaces for literacy education exist? Which spaces are publicly available? Who has access to spaces for literacy education? What is the basis for access? What costs are associated with access to spaces for literacy education?
- What reading resources are available? What is the literacy quality of the reading materials? What subjects are addressed? In what language are the reading resources? Where are they stocked? Who has access to resources? What is the basis for access? What costs are associated with accessing them, such as buying a magazine at a drugstore?
- What materials are available to support literacy, such as writing tools and surfaces?
- What literacy-related technology is available, such as hardware, software, tape recorders, cell phones, and assistive technology? What is the quality of those technologies? What technology infrastructures exist, and what is their quality, including stability? Who has access to technology and supporting infrastructure? What is the basis for access? What costs are associated with accessing them, such as buying equipment and paying for internet service?
- What community or government support is available? What is its quality? What policies support literacy and literacy education? How are those policies enforced? What funding is available for literacy and literacy education? How are decisions made concerning resource allocation?

The inventory-takers then need to identify community literacy strengths and weaknesses, including literacy gaps, such as groups of people in high need of literacy education. Matching the literacy needs and the available resources helps determine if the community has the capacity to address those literacy needs or if they need additional resources or expertise.

Probably the two most important factors are: (1) conveniently available and accessible relevant, competently written reading materials; and (2) people who teach literacy skills. To begin with, the only requirements are a handful of literate people who can teach, writing supplies, and a place to stock reading materials. Literate writers can create reading materials on paper, cloth, or other writing surface. All communities have a space to hold reading materials, even if it is a box or basket under a shelter. It is possible that no one has been specifically trained to teach literacy, so they would need that training. Fortunately, many books and guides exist regarding that skill. At the least, some educational institution or ministry should be able to provide that information in print format or as a workshop. If the community has internet connectivity, such as cell phone access, then literate people can locate online literacy training resources.

More advanced or larger communities can identify specific resource gaps and focus on acquiring those materials to address those gaps. Similarly, communities might identify specific groups that need or want literacy support, and identify what expertise is needed to target that population. For instance, refugees who do not know the local language may need reading material in their home language and teachers who can speak in their home language. Usually among the refugees is someone who can teach and someone who can speak the community's language at a basic level. Such communities can also consult government and social agencies, including libraries, for guidance. Technology, if available, can also facilitate access to appropriate teaching strategies and culturally appropriate reading materials.

These efforts assume that people in the community can work together collaboratively. Community leaders should facilitate a clear literacy vision and mission that is "owned" by the community because such literacy can benefit many community stakeholders. The inventory task helps identify the resources that each stakeholder can contribute, be it expertise, labor, space, materials, or funding. Building on each other's contributions empowers the community as a whole, including literacy learners. Community-developed policies and procedures can help make such literacy efforts sustainable. Equally as important, growing literacy competence can lead to more productivity and civic engagement, which again strengthens the community.

A community-wide effort helps create a culture of literacy (Hanemann & Krolak, 2017). In such a culture, a community-wide norm of reading exists. Literacy is considered a lifelong skill, and occurs within and across age ranges;

everyone is included in literacy education and practice. People are expected to read and write as part of their personal and workaday life. Literacy practices take place at the family, neighborhood, workplace, and community levels. The community has a variety of convenient collections of relevant, well-written reading materials covering many different topics of interest. Local book and periodical publishing are encouraged and supported. Community members share their literacy experiences and help each other advance literacy; public spaces for such interactions are common and conveniently located. People have many opportunities to practice and improve their literacy competence in socioeconomic development activities. Community laws and regulations support literacy, through education and resources, to ensure a sustainable culture of literacy.

This book provides many examples of community-based efforts to support literacy. It is possible to do in every community. Now it is time for that possibility to become a reality.

REFERENCE

Hanemann, U., & Krolak, L. (Eds.). (2017). *Fostering a culture of reading and writing: Examples of dynamic literate environments.* Hamburg, Germany: UNESCO Institute for Lifelong Learning.

Index